Then all at once he tried his wings;
the whir of them was louder than before,
and they carried him swiftly away.

—Hans Christian Andersen, "The Ugly Duckling"

PENGUIN BOOKS

SEATTLE SLEW

Steve Cady, a graduate of Harvard, has been a sports reporter
for *The New York Times* since 1960. He has also written for the
Reader's Digest and is co-author, with Robert Lipsyte, of
Something Going, a novel about horse racing published in 1973.
He admits that years ago he was one of thirty-six investors in
Pipe Dream Stable, whose single occupant was an
unremarkable runner named Miss Linley.

A graduate of Brooklyn College, Barton Silverman has been a
staff photographer for *The New York Times* since 1964. In 1971
he was New York Press Photographer of the Year, and he is
currently Vice President of the New York Press Photographers'
Association. His work has been published in more than fifty
books; has appeared in such magazines as *Life, Sports
Illustrated,* and *Newsweek;* and is represented in several
important collections, including that of New York's Museum
of Modern Art.

SEATTLE SLEW

STEVE CADY

BARTON SILVERMAN

PENGUIN BOOKS

Penguin Books Ltd, Harmondsworth,
Middlesex, England
Penguin Books, 625 Madison Avenue,
New York, New York 10022 U.S.A.
Penguin Books Australia Ltd, Ringwood,
Victoria, Australia
Penguin Books Canada Limited, 2801 John Street,
Markham, Ontario, Canada L3R 1B4
Penguin Books (N.Z.) Ltd, 182–190 Wairau Road,
Auckland 10, New Zealand

First published in the United States of America
in simultaneous hardbound and paperbound editions
by The Viking Press and Penguin Books 1977

Library of Congress Cataloging in Publication Data
Cady, Steve.
Seattle Slew.

1.   Seattle Slew (Race horse)   I.   Silverman, Barton.
II.   Title.
SF355.S416C3   798′.43   77-11969
ISBN 0 14 00.4758 1

Printed in the United States of America by Rand McNally and Company, Chicago, Illinois
Color printed by Rae Publishing Company, Inc., Cedar Grove, New Jersey.
Set in Helvetica Light   Book design by Judith Michael
With the exception of those mentioned below, all black and white photographs in
this book were taken by Barton Silverman. Color photographs, unless credited
otherwise, were also taken by Barton Silverman.

Michael Coers / Courier-Journal and Louisville Times, p. 100.
Bob Coglianese / New York Racing Association, pp. 54, 57, 61.
Jerry Cook / Sports Illustrated, p. 64.
John Cornell / Newsday, p. 136.
Billy Davis / Courier-Journal and Louisville Times, p. 101.
Dan Dry, pp. 16, 22, 23.
Fasig–Tipton, Inc., pp. 33, 39.
Harvey Cartoons, p. 45.
Bud Kamenish / Courier-Journal and Louisville Times, pp. 99, 103.
Tony Leonard, p. 14.
New York Racing Association, p. 143.
Chuck Solomon, pp. 128, 129 right.
Pam Spaulding / Courier-Journal and Louisville Times, p. 19 bottom.
Paula Turner, p. 47.
UPI, pp. 18, 97.
Bob Walker / New York Times, p. 131.
Wide World, p. 19 top.
Marilyn Yee / New York Times, p. 137.

CONTENTS

PREFACE

Once upon a time, on a cold Kentucky night, another bluegrass baby struggled to its feet.

He was an alert young horse but plain, a dark first foal with coarse features and a body that seemed out of proportion. His head was too big, his legs too long. Right from the start, the colt had trouble getting himself together. It took him nearly three times longer than usual to steady himself in the stall enough to nurse.

Fifteen months later, he was still a gangly young Thoroughbred whose legs the farm manager remembers "kind of flopped around" when he ran. At the yearling auction where he was sold, few bidders paid much attention. He was just too uncoordinated, too unfashionable, too . . . ordinary. And at the farm in Maryland where he was broken to the saddle his teacher had a nickname for the big, ungainly adolescent the minute she saw him. She took one look, stuck her hands in the back pockets of her blue jeans, and said with as much affection as candidness, "Baby Huey!"

The nickname, inspired by a clumsy but lovable comic-book duck, followed the colt to the racetrack when he became a two-year-old and was shipped to Belmont Park in New York. There, his name shortened to Huey, he was ridden by nearly everyone around the barn at one time or another during his first few months of big-bellied jogs and leisurely gallops.

Like the fairy-tale Ugly Duckling, Huey was good-tempered. He didn't have a mean bone in his body. But when he galloped, his hoofs would hit the ground heavily with a kal-umph, kal-umph sound, and the stablehands wondered if he'd ever make it as a racehorse. He was such a klutz he seemed at times to have five legs. One morning in early April, when the weather turned warmer and the crocuses began to appear, his trainer decided to give Huey his first taste of real running.

"We have to get this guy started sometime," Billy Turner told his exercise rider. "Breeze him three-eighths of a mile. No big deal."

Now, for the first time under saddle, Huey would be moving from a natural gallop into a faster, longer stride that approached racing speed. To help in his transition, a seasoned older stablemate would run with him: a routine gallop of half a mile or so, then the breeze. Huey just galloped along awkwardly as usual, not taking hold of the bit and not seeming particularly interested in what he was doing. But then the exercise rider put the reins together, chirped for speed—and got what he says was the biggest shock of his eighteen-year career on the racetrack.

"Huey just put his head in the air," Mike Kennedy remembers, "and opened his mouth so wide you could have thrown a baby in there. He took hold of that bit and started running away from that older horse and I thought, 'What the hell is going on here?' "

When Mike finally pulled him up, Huey turned around and started snorting and blowing. All of a sudden he had been asked to run, and he had found he could do something he enjoyed. He wanted to run and never stop. And he never did.

While the skeptics waited for him to be exposed as a fraud, Huey continued crossing them up. When his rivals pushed him, he broke track records, and when they couldn't, he coasted home far in front as nonchalantly as a saddle horse out for a riding-academy canter. And finally, on a rare June day in 1977, the three-year-old colt now known around the world as Seattle Slew became the first undefeated horse in racing history to sweep the Triple Crown: the Kentucky Derby, the Preakness, and the Belmont Stakes. In nine races over a nine-month span, he had won at distances from three-quarters of a mile to a mile and a half, always with speed in reserve. Nine earlier Triple Crown winners, from Sir Barton to Secretariat, had earned the red roses, black-eyed Susans, and white carnations. But none had accomplished the sweep with an unblemished record.

He was famous now, a $17,500 yearling who had emerged from a public auction to become the world's most valuable animal. His owners, the people who had seen promise in a plain-looking colt, were weighing offers as high as twelve million dollars for their horse's syndication as a breeding stallion.

But none of those financial deliberations concerned Huey. All he wanted to do was run. His legs had wings, the wings of a fairy-tale swan, and they had carried him swiftly away.

SECRET AT SARATOGA

Hope begins at dawn on the racetrack, rising with the sun to the wake-up call of a rooster. Horses poke their heads out of cell-block stalls and wait for the liberation of a walk, a gallop, or a race. Stablehands, reassuring them in a language that only animals understand, dream of the big horse who will carry the stable to the top of the world.

By the middle of the third week in August of 1956, the secret was out. Before long, it would be all over the racetrack. People sworn to silence would be babbling to strangers. Even the dogs in the stable area at Saratoga would be barking it: "Billy Turner has a Bold Reasoning colt in his barn that can fly."

Nobody knew the horse's name. They only knew that he had worked three-quarters of a mile one August morning in "ten and one," which is clocker jargon for 1 minute 10 1/5 seconds. And, as everyone knows, unraced two-year-olds don't have workouts that fast. Not even at Saratoga, the dowager queen of American race-tracks, where the best old families and best young horses have been spending their Augusts since 1863.

"Sure I've got a colt who went in ten and one," joked Turner, the mystery horse's trainer, giving the snoopers his most disingenuous shrug. "But he worked five-eighths, not three-quarters. Shucks, anyone can do that."

When they sidled up to Mike Kennedy, the colt's exercise rider, he shook his head and laughed his best Irish laugh and said, "Are you crazy? You know maiden two-year-olds don't work that fast."

But Billy and Mike, both from a steeplechasing background that makes horsemen wise, knew what they had. So did Dr. Jim Hill, the veterinarian who looked after the health of the horses Turner trained, and so did Jean Cruguet, the jockey, and most of the stablehands. It was Huey, formerly Baby Huey, the same clumsy colt they had known since he arrived at Belmont Park six months

1

earlier. Except that Huey wasn't a klutz any more. He was putting it together at Saratoga, getting smoother and stronger, taking the bit between his teeth and leaning against it. He wanted to run.

Early in the third week of Saratoga's 109th meeting, the people closest to the Bold Reasoning colt were wondering how long the secret could last. The clockers weren't putting the results of the workouts in the paper, for some reason. But the racetrack had eyes and ears, thousands of them.

Take the Squirrel, for instance. The previous week on August 11, when Mike had worked Huey five-eighths of a mile in 58 2/5 seconds on swampy grass at the training center known as Oklahoma, the Squirrel had seen Billy Turner stand straight up on his stable pony and put his hands in the air to slow them down.

"Who was *that*?" he had shouted at the trainer, running across the wet grass.

"You'll read about this one, Jimmy," Turner had said, riding off. He had known the Squirrel, a former exercise rider named Jimmy Weininger, for several years. He also knew that the Squirrel was custodian of the press box at Saratoga, Belmont Park, and Aqueduct, the three tracks operated by the New York Racing Association. Still, the next day's *Daily Racing Form* provided only a misleading clue to Huey's identity. The work tab credited a five-furlong breeze on the grass to Seattle Sue, obviously the name of a filly, and the time was listed as 1:00 2/5 instead of 58 2/5 seconds. Except for a handful of insiders, the racing fraternity apparently still didn't know that Huey's official name was Seattle Slew, or that he was owned by Karen and Mickey Taylor of White Swan, Washington.

And for some reason, the six-furlong workout of 1:10 1/5 would *never* appear in the *Racing Form*, even though clockers normally pay more attention when they see a jockey instead of an exercise rider on a horse's back. Cruguet, the French jockey whom some trainers admired and others did not, had breezed Huey once about a month earlier at Belmont Park. Today was the second time.

The choice of Cruguet as the horse's jockey pleased Kennedy. Earlier in the summer, when they knew what Huey could do, the exercise rider had encouraged Turner to keep letting him work the horse instead of putting a jockey up. "We can kill the country with this horse," Kennedy, never one to miss a chance to cash a bet,

Steamboat and
Billy Turner
escorting Seattle Slew
and Jean Cruguet
to a 1977
morning workout.
Right:
Jimmy Weininger
(the Squirrel)
in the Belmont
press box.

3

had said. "Putting a jockey on him now will only attract the clockers."

But when Huey worked so fast on the grass, skimming along so easily along the soggy surface, Turner had decided it was time to start thinking about a jockey. The horse was getting close to a race. There was a race in the condition book for two-year-old maidens (nonwinners) on the closing day of the meeting, August 28, and that could be the spot for his debut. Would his regular jockey be Eddie Maple, a competent journeyman who rode a lot for Turner? Would it be one of the popular Spanish-speaking riders, like Angel Cordero or Jorge Velasquez? Or would it be Cruguet? At the age of thirty-six, the French jockey was at a crossroads in his career, just back after an illness, not much in demand, and now associated with a new agent, Oliver Cutshaw. Like everybody else, Cutshaw and Cruguet were looking for a big horse.

Turner and Kennedy talked about Cruguet's weak reputation among some of the trainers, about his alleged interest in betting, about the fact that he was not regarded as a good whip rider or a good gate rider.

"I know all that," Kennedy said, "but he's got dynamite hands. All you need is somebody with a good pair of hands who will sit still and relax him, keep him balanced with a long hold. Billy, this horse doesn't need anybody jumping up and down on him whipping the ass off of him. He's going to run his eyeballs out anyway. You need somebody to sit still."

"You know, Mike," the trainer said, "maybe you're right. Maybe the Frenchman would fit this horse better than anybody else."

Turner and Kennedy shared a common steeplechasing background in horse racing, though their careers had developed on opposite sides of the ocean. Turner, thirty-six years old, grew up around horses in the Unionville section of southern Pennsylvania. At seventeen, he entered Emory College in Atlanta but he rode steeplechasers on weekends for W. Burling (Burley) Cocks. Then he was a 105-pound jockey only five feet five inches tall, but two years later they were calling him "Jockey Toolong" and his future as a contestant was coming apart for he had grown to nearly his present height of six feet two. In 1976, after years of groundwork with the jumpers as assistant trainer for Cocks, Turner was in his tenth full season as a head trainer in flat racing.

Soft-spoken and easygoing, with a deft way of turning a phrase, he felt most comfortable in the tweed caps and turtleneck jerseys favored by the steeplechase set.

He also preferred words like "gosh" and "shucks" and "oh my goodness" to the coarser language used by many racetrackers. But if the mild words suggested a wide-eyed innocence, the impression was deceptive. Billy Turner, a thoroughly schooled horseman from way back, didn't miss a trick.

Neither did Mike Kennedy, his top exercise rider for the last four seasons and one of his closest confidants. For Kennedy, thirty-eight, the racetrack trail went back to Waterford, Ireland, near the southeast coast, where he quit school at fifteen to become a groom, exercise rider, and apprentice jockey. Later on, after a stay in England, he spent three years as a regular steeplechase jockey in Ireland. When he came to the United States in the mid-1960s, he had already worked for some of the best trainers in racing, including Vincent O'Brien and Paddy Pendergast. But if horses were his first love, they were only his secondary source of income in New York. His important paychecks came from his job as a pari-mutuel clerk, selling and cashing tickets at New York tracks. Being an exercise rider meant getting up at 5:15 a.m., taking naps later in the morning, and going to bed early. But the extra two hundred a week helped him support his wife and two young daughters, and, besides, horses were part of his life.

Free-lance exercise boys, who usually made about four dollars a horse and up to twice that for rogues and problem cases that nobody else wanted to ride, could make more than a salaried rider if they hustled. But the blue-eyed, 130-pound Irishman preferred his salaried status and the chance it gave him to work with the same horses every day. He had been on some decent ones in Europe, even a couple of English Derby winners, but none had given him the feeling of competence that Huey projected. This colt ran like a deer, gliding and floating along as if he were on springs. He did things effortlessly, so smoothly that it was unreal. Kennedy thought back to the day in February when Huey arrived at Belmont after being broken to the saddle in Maryland by Paula Turner, Billy's wife.

"What do you think of this guy?" Billy had said, calling him over to a stall.

Mike's reaction to the newcomer, who was so big and ungainly

John Polston, Slew's groom, applying standing bandages.

5

and common-looking, was: "Turner, where in the hell did you get this horse? This guy is going to take ten years to get to the races."

"Well," said the trainer, "at least if he can't run, he can pull a milk wagon."

But Huey had fooled them both. And after the breeze in April, when they discovered he could run, Turner did what an unusually patient trainer always does with a promising young horse: nothing. For the next two months, until June, Huey was never asked for speed again. He was just allowed to gallop easily, a mile or two a day, growing and muscling out and not hurting himself. Turner knew he had a racehorse.

And now, by the third week of the Saratoga meeting, so did the whole barn. It had not been a particularly happy meeting for the Turner outfit, stabled in the Horse Haven section of the Oklahoma training area across Union Avenue from the racetrack. None of the trainer's sixteen horses, most of them two-year-olds and most of them owned by Milton Ritzenberg, had won a race at the meeting. Only a few had even been to the post. To make matters worse, the previous week, the stable's big horse, a three-year-old named Lord Henribee, at one time a Derby hopeful, had died after being stricken with founder, a disorder affecting the limbs. But race-trackers learn to take the bad with the good. Chicken today, feathers tomorrow. And Turner's troops, on the morning of Huey's six-furlong workout, had turned out cheerfully in the early mist, breathing the fresh country air and smelling the new-mown hay.

As usual, a girl called Sam, a college graduate whose formal name of Debra Goldman gave way to the nickname when she came onto the racetrack as a groom, was doing her best to keep the hired hands smiling. "Are you sure you're kosher, John?" she called out to Huey's groom, John Polston, as the thirty-two-year-old black man emerged from a stall. "I have to know." When Billy Turner made an ambiguous reference to women's lib, Sam shook her head and said, "Are you causing trouble again, Turner? You're fired already. I fired you half a dozen times today."

When it came to employer-employee relations, Turner had always operated with a loose rein rather than a Captain Bligh approach. The people who work for him respond by working harder and more efficiently than they would for a sterner taskmaster.

One of the "secrets" of Turner's training program has been to give the horse a chance to hack or take light exercise around Belmont's miles of paths in the early morning. Here Cruguet gives Slew, an inquisitive horse by nature, a chance to check out a collie and its owner. Left: Debra Goldman and John Polston relaxing between chores.

6

For Sam, a twenty-two-year-old biology major who used to ask for horse models instead of dolls when she was a girl, the track was a pleasant way-station on a journey to somewhere else. Her presence reflected a growing trend on the backstretch: greater numbers of young women, most of them from comfortable middle-class families, finding fulfillment as grooms, hot-walkers, and exercise riders. Like many of the others, a group that accounted for about a fourth of the stable help, she came to the racetrack after years of riding-academy and horse-show experience. She was a groom now, caring for four horses and occasionally working as an exercise rider. Before Huey began getting too strong for the girls, she had ridden him in easy gallops, following the advice of Mike Kennedy: "He's no problem, just don't be messing with his head because he likes to be left alone." She remembered the big colt from Belmont as a docile mount who didn't buck or grab the bit or try to run off, the way some high-strung racehorses do. Sam tended to feel that a price tag could never be put on work in the insulated world of the backstretch, with its kaleidoscope of life styles. With horses your day never ended. You had to like them or you might just as well be in an office.

John Polston, with a wife and two growing boys to support, saw it differently. It took years, he knew, to develop the special skills and feeling needed to keep a horse at its best. Yet the people with that know-how were the serfs in a feudalistic racing kingdom. Stablehands earned less than anyone else in racing, less even than the men who came around on the compost trucks to take away the straw bedding from the concrete manure pits outside each barn. And for a black man, Polston had found, rising on the racetrack to anything higher than stablehand was particularly tough. The only way to survive was to take your chances at the pari-mutuel windows. If you knew when a horse was good, if you had the right information on the right horse, you could maybe make yourself a hundred or two and fatten the weekly paycheck.

Like Turner and Kennedy, Polston came up through the steeplechase route, spending five years with Mike Smithwick, a trainer he went to work for at the age of sixteen in Maryland after quitting school when his grandmother died. With more than fifteen years at the trade, he had no trouble getting a job in Turner's barn the previous winter, about the time Huey arrived. Polston had always preferred working with colts, because he liked to move

8

around on both sides of the horse. He considered fillies more flighty and temperamental, like women in general. In March, when the only colt he had was sent back to the farm, he took over as Huey's groom.

"I had my eye on him," he would confess, "because one day when he had a high fever, he was raising the devil, real playful. Usually when a horse is carrying a fever, he's in the stall with his head down."

So Polston had kept his eye on Huey, and the others had, too. They knew he might be a good one, the kind of horse who could win a bet for you or make an even bigger dream come true. It wasn't just that the colt had shown he could run. Some horses burn up the track in workouts and die in the afternoon when the money is on the line, just morning glories-that can't stand the heat of competition. Some of them get nervous if they're near the rail; others don't like to be on the outside. Some have courage when they're in front listening to the cadence of their own hoofbeats, yet turn to jelly when another horse looks them in the eye.

But Huey did things so effortlessly that the people around him felt they had something going. And on that August morning at Saratoga they were looking forward to his workout. It would not be the kind of clandestine work that takes place at dawn or even in pre-dawn murkiness. Huey was still in his stall as the morning wound down and the stablehands entered the home stretch of their busy routine. It was nearly 10 a.m. and the sun, hot now, was high in the sky. Huey stared at another horse being led around the barn slowly on a cooling-out walk by Donald Carroll, a twenty-one-year-old hot-walker from Elmont, Long Island. Donald, a soft-spoken young man, had a way with horses. He and Huey already had established a close rapport.

At a nearby barn, a groom on a coffee break patted a gentle-looking beagle lying under a sign that read "Beware Bad Dog." As stablehands turned to polishing the tack, the smell of saddle soap mingled with wintergreen and the musky aroma of horses, hay, and oats. The horses, given their two quarts of breakfast oats at 4:30 a.m. by the night watchman, would be having lunch soon. On the mini-clotheslines strung from the edges of the shed-row roofs, horse bandages and old rub-rags and T-shirts stirred in the warm sunlight.

In stable offices, trainers who had sent out their last horses of

the morning were on the phone, reassuring owners that this horse had worked well or that that horse was nearly ready for a race or that some other horse, a chronic loser, would be dropped down real quick to get rid of him. The jockey agents, hustling through the stable area earlier in cars or on foot, were beginning to ease up, putting away their dog-eared condition books that tell what races are coming up two weeks in advance. Even the clockers had begun to relax their grips on the stopwatches when Turner told John Polston, "Get Huey ready." The colt would be the last horse of the day in Turner's barn to go out. He would be heading down a sandy path that would take him out of the Horse Haven complex, across Union Avenue at the place where Pinkerton guards stop the cars, and onto the main track.

Turner led the way on Steamboat, a brown and white six-year-old stable pony who already had become Huey's buddy. Sam told people that the pony was part Percheron and part Clydesdale, but his mixed pedigree could really be traced to pinto ancestors. Thanks to his broad beam, which inspired his nickname, he made a comfortable command post for Turner. But Steam, as he was called around the barn, had an unfortunate habit of crossing his front feet when he tried to gallop too fast. So Turner never sent him out in the afternoon to take any of the horses to the post for a race. The thing Steam could do better than anything else was eat. On a recent day, he had broken out of his stall and headed straight for an open sack of oats at the end of the shed row. When one of the stablehands went after him, Steam grabbed the ninety-pound sack in his teeth and ran out of the barn with it.

Riding to the main track now, Turner reflected on how lucky they had been that the colt had remained as sound as a dollar. Now he was nearly ready to race. Turner was aware of the old racetrack saying, "Nobody with an untried two-year-old in the barn ever committed suicide." He understood.

Every day, at racetracks all over the world, untried two-year-olds go out in the morning for their workouts, yet few of them ever fulfill the hope held for them. Nearly sixty thousand Thoroughbreds race each year in the United States and Canada, and about fifty thousand of those do not earn enough to meet the annual expenses of ten thousand dollars or more.

But still, Turner thought, there was a special kind of magic about those untried two-year-olds, especially the young horses that bloomed like buds each summer at Saratoga. Some of the best horses in history had made their first or second starts at the nation's oldest racetrack, a glamorous anachronism that probably comes as close as any American track to presenting racing as it deserves to be presented. As usual, some of the most promising two-year-olds were on the grounds that August morning. C. V. Whitney's Banquet Table, already a stakes winner, was being pointed for the Hopeful on closing day. LeRoy Jolley, getting Honest Pleasure ready for the historic Travers Stakes coming up on Saturday, had a good-looking full brother of that beaten Kentucky Derby favorite in his barn, a two-year-old named For the Moment. The younger colt had recently won a maiden race and would be moving up to tougher company. Another young prospect, Sanhedrin, a Darby Dan Farm colt trained by Lou Rondinello and bred for distance, also had left the maiden ranks before shipping to the upstate New York track.

People would pay almost any price for a horse they thought could take them to the top. Just the previous week, at the annual Saratoga Yearling Sales, a colt by Secretariat had gone for $550,000. The Taylors had been in town for the sale, but they were back in Washington now. Meanwhile, here was Huey, the colt they bought as a yearling for $17,500, marching onto the track with his ears up, listening, muscles rippling under the dark brown coat. Cruguet jogged him down past the stands, decked out in their masses of red geraniums and white petunias, past the clubhouse porch where the dawdlers in the breakfast crowd were finishing up their bacon and eggs and digging into their Hand melons. In a little while, the last of the dishes would be cleared away, the workouts would end, and the track would be prepared for another languid afternoon of racing. Thoughts were already turning to the afternoon action, as copies of the *Racing Form* were opened and studied. Somewhere in the sprawling stable area, nine new winners were waiting to be discovered by the handicappers.

Down at the rail, Doc Hill kept his eyes on the Bold Reasoning colt. John Polston had come over with Donald Carroll's younger brother, Dennis, the assistant trainer, who was checking his stopwatch. Up in the stands, Mike Kennedy watched with Denise Cruguet, the jockey's wife. Cruguet chirped to Huey on the backstretch and the colt sprang forward, accelerating with easy strides.

"He's just galloping," Kennedy told Denise Cruguet as the colt came past the finish line. "Probably twelve and change, maybe thirteen. He was going real easy."

But once again, Huey had fooled the exercise rider. Kennedy had failed to notice Billy Turner, standing up once more on Steamboat and waving his arms, this time at Cruguet, in a frantic slow-down signal. But the Squirrel, on the scene again, hadn't missed it. When Doc Hill asked a man with a stopwatch how he timed the colt, the man said, "Ten and one. Never saw a horse get it that easy."

Back at the barn, when Polston told Donald and Sam the news, Sam shook her head and said, "That couldn't be it, tell me the right time."

But as Polston washed the colt down after the workout, he whispered into his ear: "You're not a baby any more, Huey. You're Hugo now. I'm gonna call you Hugo."

To Paula Turner, though, the colt was still Huey. She hadn't seen his workout, because she had been coming back from the track on another horse. But Huey's time hadn't surprised her.

That afternoon at the track, lighting a mentholated cigarette, Cruguet told his agent Cutshaw, a former jockey and trainer, "Don't mess up the book, Oliver. Billy Turner has a good maiden, so make sure you don't get another call on a race."

Later in the afternoon, Doc Hill called Mickey Taylor at his trailer home in White Swan, a little logging community 140 miles southeast of Seattle in the middle of the Yakima Indian reservation.

"Mick," the veterinarian said, "we've got a colt that's something special."

And Billy Turner, who had been waiting ten years for a horse that could laugh at the world, was beginning to wonder if he had found him at last. Many months later, the trainer would tell interviewers, "You can't buy horses like this. You can't breed 'em and you can't steal 'em. One day you just look up, and there it is." On that August night in 1976, the thought was already taking shape in Turner's mind. He didn't know much about Huey's background. But he knew he had found an exceptional horse, a horse that was different from any other he had ever trained. It was a gratifying feeling, but a little scary.

Mike Kennedy is more than just Slew's exercise rider. He has been closely involved with his development as a racehorse and feels an affection for the animal that goes far beyond the call of routine duty.

12

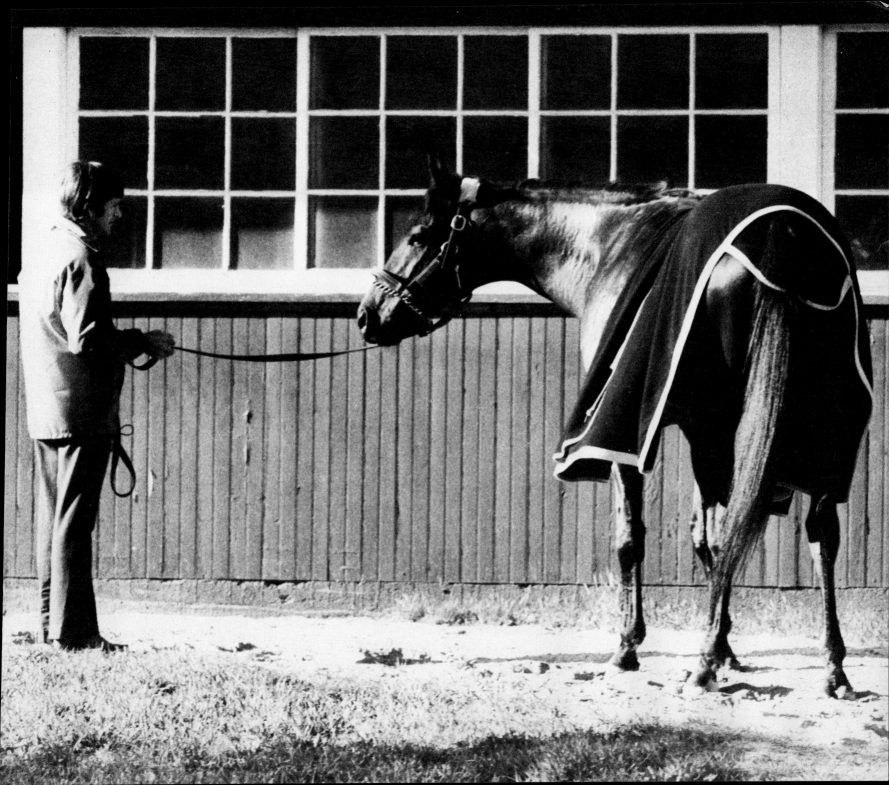

BIRTH OF A DARK HORSE

Paul Mallory had warned his wife at supper that it might be a busy night. After six years as the manager of Ben S. Castleman's horse-breeding farm, Mallory knew when a brood mare's time was near. And My Charmer, a five-year-old bay mare with a modest racing record but a sweet disposition, had been telling her forty-nine-year-old keeper all day long that she was about to become a mother.

The first clue came when she went off by herself to the back of the field, away from the other brood mares. Then she started fence-walking, nervously pacing back and forth alongside the creosote-darkened oak railings that enclose the meadows and paddocks of Castleman's White Horse Acres beside the Newtown Pike in Lexington, Kentucky. She would go to the feed tub but only take a single bite, and then she would walk some more.

At 3:30 p.m., Mallory put her into a brood-mare barn on a gently rising slope that overlooks the hundred-acre farm. At 5 p.m., he moved her into the double-sized foaling stall at the end of the barn and went to supper while his eighteen-year-old daughter, Ann, and a solicitous black Labrador named Trouble stood watch. Mallory returned an hour later, switched on a portable television set in the tiny lookout room next to a screened window in the wall of the foaling stall—and waited. He knew it wouldn't be long.

As darkness settled over the bluegrass country and the temperature dipped below freezing, Christine Mallory rushed to finish the supper chores and hurried through the winter night to join her husband and daughter. Walking the hundred yards from her white frame house to the barn, she thought of the days when she used to work as a nurse's aide in a hospital delivery room. When it came to babies, she felt, brood mares weren't much different from women. They all had the same feelings.

"Let the mare do the work," she reminded her daughter a little later as My Charmer's contractions grew stronger and the front

Seattle Slew
as a foal
with Paul Mallory,
manager of
White Horse Acres.

15

feet and head of the foal began to appear. "Let nature take its course."

With Paul Mallory holding one front leg of the foal, his wife the other, and Ann cradling the head to keep it from sagging, My Charmer knew exactly what to do. It was an easy, routine birth, unusually so for a first foal. Eleven months after a clinically brief date with a new sire named Bold Reasoning at nearby Claiborne Farm, My Charmer had foaled a baby colt at the convenient hour of 7 o'clock on the night of February 15, 1974. It was almost as if she knew there were other mares waiting to use the foaling stall.

A few minutes after the foal was born, Christine Mallory thought: Maybe this will be it, maybe this one will be a Derby winner. Over the years, she had seen so many newborn racehorses she had lost count, yet each time a new foal arrived, she would think of it as a possible Derby winner. They never were, and she doubted it would be any different for the dark colt now gawking inquisitively at the world from his thick bed of straw. Even to Christine Mallory's sympathetic eye, this one didn't *look* like a winner. The head seemed coarse and large, out of proportion, and the legs looked awkwardly long even by the leggy standards of newborn foals. His dark body bore no stars or blazes or other patches of white that would distinguish him from other horses. In short, he was a fairly homely baby. And right now, he was getting in the way of maternity-ward progress.

Another mare needed the foaling stall, so My Charmer and her son were transferred to smaller quarters. There, still under close surveillance, the foal spent nearly an hour wobbling around trying to steady himself in order to nurse. Each time he reached his mother's side, he would lunge past her and brush against the sides of the stall.

No matter, Christine Mallory thought. Every new foal was a thrilling event. And maybe this one, somehow, would become good enough to run for the roses in the 1977 Kentucky Derby at Churchill Downs in Louisville, sixty-five miles west of White Horse Acres. After all, wasn't he a great-grandson of the fabled Bold Ruler, the father of Secretariat? Furthermore, his mother's side of the family traced back to Myrtle Charm, the champion two-year-old filly of 1948, and before that to Myrtlewood, the amazing mare of the 1930s who broke track records, beat colts, and foaled seven famous daughters.

Mr. and Mrs. Castleman
at the farm.

17

Bold Reasoning,
Seattle Slew's sire.

Even so, the odds against My Charmer's baby ever making a name for himself would be astronomical. He would be one of nearly thirty thousand Thoroughbreds foaled in North America that winter and spring, she knew, and the road from the breeding shed to the winner's circle would be a hazardous one. He had survived the first hazard, the occasional miscarriage. But his right leg, which appeared to turn outward slightly, could become crooked. He could be injured by the hooves of a playmate, cripple himself on a fence, become neurotic if other horses rejected or bullied him, or even be killed by a bolt of lightning while standing under an unrodded tree. Or, as so often happens, he could get to the races and not be able to run much faster than a pet saddle horse. Breeding racehorses on your own for profit, Castleman and Mallory knew, made drilling for oil seem like a safe investment. But the game continued.

As Mallory had predicted, it turned out to be a busy Friday night, the busiest night ever at White Horse Acres. Everything happened very quickly. A second foal was born at 8:30, a third just before midnight. Of the two dozen mares on the farm that year, only My Charmer and three others belonged to Castleman. The rest were boarders. But the boarders received the same loving attention as the others, and Mallory didn't get to bed until 4 o'clock in the morning. He was up again two hours later, convinced once more that horses needed lots more care than the tobacco he used to farm. This was the busiest time of year for him, since Thoroughbred foals start arriving in late January and most are born in February, March, or April. Because for racing purposes all Thoroughbreds become a year older on January 1, an April or May foal is considered a late one, though latecomers have managed on rare occasion to win the Derby and other classics for three-year-olds.

My Charmer's colt was outdoors the day after he was born, all legs and eyes and twitching tail, walking and trotting alongside his mother as if pulled by an invisible string. It was a scene that was taking place at breeding farms in every state of the Union as the annual search for another Triple Crown winner got under way. The familiar cycle had begun: the first foals of what would be a class of nearly twenty-nine thousand were starting to hit the ground, only one of them destined to win the 1977 Derby. Last

Sunny Jim
Fitzsimmons
with Bold Ruler,
Slew's famous
great-grandfather.

My Charmer,
running with
Slew's younger
half brother
by Jacinto.
She is now owned
by Hermitage Farm
in Goshen, Kentucky,
and is in foal
to Secretariat.

year's foals were beginning to fill out as yearlings; more than seven thousand stallions and fifty-five thousand brood mares were warming up for a February-to-June breeding season that would produce the winner of the 1978 Derby. Money and patience were the prime requisites for playing the game, and hope was the chief by-product.

Some people raise their own horses, called homebreds, to carry the family silks. Some, known as market breeders, simply raise Thoroughbreds for market on a cash-crop basis, much as other men raise corn or cattle. And some, like Ben Castleman, do a little of both. My Charmer's son, Mallory knew, was slated to be sold at auction after about a year and a half on the farm. Castleman made it a practice to sell his colts as yearlings and to keep the fillies for racing and eventual brood-mare service.

By bluegrass standards, White Horse Acres was a very modest layout, hardly larger than some of the pastures on showplaces such as six-thousand-acre Claiborne Farm in Paris, Kentucky, twelve miles away. Castleman, a sixty-eight-year-old restaurateur, had been interested in horses most of his life. As owner of the White Horse Tavern in northern Kentucky near Cincinnati, he had fed and entertained horsemen and horseplayers for more than thirty years. But he didn't buy his first racehorse until 1955, and he didn't buy White Horse Acres until 1967, paying $92,000 for the original sixty-nine-acre farm. His foundation mare was Fair Charmer, the mother of My Charmer. Since Castleman had no stallions of his own, he operated by sending his mares to available sires whose stud fees he could afford.

Horse breeders, the ones who make a science out of it, pore over pedigree charts going back six generations to weigh the speed or staying ability of prospective parents and scribble equations in their notebooks: S (this sire) times D (that dam) equals X. All of them are looking for the unborn X who will turn out to be the big horse, the horse whose exploits can turn a deficit-ridden operation into a winner. For those who even come close to the ultimate equation, the rewards are great. But few come close. Even when they do, Mallory knew, it wasn't always the result of breeding the best to the best and hoping for the best, the credo of racing's leading breeders. Breeding racehorses was an inexact science at best, which was what made it so intriguing.

The mating that produced My Charmer's colt, Mallory suspected, may have been as much a matter of expediency as clairvoyance. He knew that his boss had wanted to breed the mare to Jacinto, one of twenty-five sires at Claiborne Farm, after she returned to White Horse Acres in December of 1972 from a two-year racing career. But Seth Hancock, the young master of Claiborne, pointed out that Jacinto's date book for the 1973 season was full.

"What else might be good?" Castleman asked the Claiborne matchmaker, adding quickly, "that I can afford."

Hancock said he'd call back. His recommendation: Bold Reasoning, a brand-new stallion just getting ready for his first breeding season. On a world-famous farm where stud fees of $25,000 or more for fashionable sires were routine, the price was right: $5000.

"Fine," said Castleman. Later, he modestly would never claim any credit for arranging the match.

What had been arranged was a mating between an unproven sire and an unproven dam, a kind of blind date involving unknown factors. Bold Reasoning, a big, fast grandson of Bold Ruler, was a late-developing colt, bothered by leg and throat ailments that kept him from making his racing debut until March of his three-year-old season. But he won his first seven races, including the Withers mile and the Jersey Derby. As a four-year-old in 1972, the bay colt set a track record of 1:08 4/5 for six furlongs at Belmont Park before the recurring throat disorder began catching up with him. He was retired at the end of that season, with a record showing eight firsts in twelve starts and earnings of $189,564.

My Charmer had been much busier, if less spectacular, at the racetrack. She carried Castleman's silks thirty-two times at the ages of two and three, winning six races but earning only $34,133. She began her racing career as a $10,000 claimer, meaning she could have been taken away from Castleman for that price by another owner. The debut came in a three-furlong "baby" race during February of 1971 at the Fair Grounds in New Orleans. She finished second, and eventually ran seven more times for a claiming tag. Her biggest moment came in the spring of her three-year-old season when she won the 1⅛-mile Fair Grounds Oaks.

My Charmer kept the date with Bold Reasoning, her first and his

third, in March of 1973. Now in February 1974 she was out in the frozen fields of White Horse Acres, with the result of that union jogging by her side.

When he was twenty-eight days old, My Charmer's son suffered the usual traumatic experience undergone by all foals whose mothers are bred back to another stallion. My Charmer suddenly disappeared, having been shipped to Claiborne Farm again for another date, this time with Jacinto. But she was back at White Horse Acres within a few hours, nuzzling her baby as if she had never been away. By mid-April, eight weeks after his birth, the Bold Reasoning colt was eating out of his own feed tub, but he and the other sucklings would stay close to their mothers until they were weaned in the fall.

Mallory calls his young horses "my babies," and they get to know and love him. But he doesn't coddle them, because he doesn't believe in raising "hothouse" horses that stay in the barn too much. For the first couple of months, the brood mares and their babies are taken into the barn at night, but when the warmer weather comes, they remain out in the fields day and night, rain or shine.

The 100th Kentucky Derby was run on the first Saturday of May that year, won by Cannonade, like Bold Reasoning a grandson of Bold Ruler. My Charmer's baby was twelve weeks old and growing fast. Through the spring and summer, in the tranquil surroundings of the farm, he and the others thrived as they ran beside mothers whose bellies already were beginning to swell with next year's foals. The Bold Reasoning colt, still awkward in Mallory's view, had grown from seventy pounds at birth to nearly four hundred pounds by the time he was weaned in early October. The separation, as usual, was harder on mother than child. My Charmer, taken to a field at the back of the farm, ran the fences and whinnied for nearly two days. Her son, in a familiar pasture with buddies who hadn't yet been weaned, hollered for a couple of hours but then rejoined the gang without a backward glance.

By January 1 of 1975, when the weanlings officially became yearlings, the colt weighed nearly seven hundred pounds. Now the colts and fillies were separated in different fields, and the muffled drumming of hoofbeats became louder as the yearling colts increased their roughhousing. Testing their legs and lungs, the yearlings would race along together and then veer like a gust of wind to avoid a fence or each other. Watching the Bold Reasoning colt, Mallory thought: He's not a graceful horse. The others run so easily that it makes him look worse. He's like a seven-foot basketball player who's only sixteen years old, too big and tall for his age.

But the colt had a good disposition. He got along well with the others, neither bullying nor allowing himself to be bullied. He just liked to play. There was one thing about him, however, that made Mallory take notice. At chow time, when the big outdoor troughs were filled with cracked corn, oats, and sweetfeed, the farm manager could always count on My Charmer's son to be first in line. As soon as he heard the feed tubs rattling, even from the far end of the thirteen-acre field, his ears would prick up and he would start running. He always got there first. Paul Mallory, busy with a new crop of foals, never really decided whether it was the heart of a champion or the stomach of a glutton that propelled him so swiftly.

Whatever the case, the answer would not be long in coming. With their second springtime on the farm drawing to a close, the yearling colts owned by Castleman were nearly ready to go to market. The owner nominated My Charmer's colt for the nearby Keeneland Summer Sales, a blue-chip auction rivaled only by the Saratoga Yearling Sales of Fasig-Tipton for fashionable merchandise. But Keeneland rejected the colt, noting that he wasn't an outstanding-looking individual and that his pedigree, showing an unproven sire and dam, wasn't all that good. That left Fasig-Tipton of Kentucky, a bargain-basement auction inaugurated in Lexington the previous year by the New York-based company, as the logical alternative.

On the afternoon of May 2, the day before the 101st Derby, My Charmer's yearling son was inspected by Ted Bates of Fasig-Tipton. The general manager of the new sale noticed right away that the colt did not have a particularly attractive head. It was coarse rather than sculpted, plain and workmanlike rather than handsome. But racehorses don't run on their heads, and the inspector paid little attention. What interested him more was the impression of strength, balance, and quickness the young horse projected.

It took Bates less than five minutes to complete his check list, marking the card quickly as the yearling first stood and then was

Left:
Seth Hancock,
master of
Claiborne Farm,
the man who
suggested
Bold Reasoning
as a mate
for My Charmer.
Right:
Paul Mallory,
the manager of
White Horse Acres,
overlooking a
group of mares.

walked back and forth in front of the barn. The confidential report Bates filed later at the office would note: "Above average in size . . . shoulder developed well . . . good angle and strong back . . . good through middle, with good spring of rib . . . nice hind leg, but passes close at hocks . . . quick appearance . . . turns out moderately right front from knee down." A rider to the report pointed out that the conformational defect in the right front leg, known as toeing out, "should not preclude a racing career."

The next day, still another Bold Ruler grandson, Foolish Pleasure, won the Derby. Two weeks later, Castleman received word that his Bold Ruler great-grandson had been accepted for the Fasig-Tipton of Kentucky Sale on July 19, to be held at a pavilion only a mile and a half down the road from White Horse Acres. The colt's grades had been excellent—a "strong 6" for conformation, a 7 for pedigree, based on a perfect score of 10. Castleman told Mallory that he had decided to let the yearling go if he brought a bid of $15,000 or more. Otherwise, the breeder intended to bid him back himself and race him with a partner from Cincinnati.

Meanwhile, the colt went back into the yearling field to run and play. Bold Reasoning was dead by this time, fatally injured in a breeding-shed accident a month earlier. My Charmer had a new foal by her side, a colt by Jacinto, and had been bred to Jacinto again. But for her first son, the idyllic days of breeding-farm tranquillity were about to end. Ahead lay the auction ring, and beyond that the demanding trail to the racetrack, a trail to gold and glory—or to failure.

John Polston
and Karen Taylor
with Seattle Slew

Right:
Slew being walked
by Mike Kennedy
and Dr. Hill
at Hialeah

Overleaf:
The Flamingo
at Hialeah.

SOLD!

How much would a rich man pay for a yearling he knew was going to become racing's first undefeated Triple Crown winner? A million dollars? Five million? Ten? Untested year-old racehorses have brought as much as a million and a half in recent years. But Seattle Slew, the only horse sold at public auction to win the Triple Crown, caused little excitement among the bidders. John Finney, president of the New York–based Fasig-Tipton Company, was the announcer, Ralph Retler the auctioneer. The action, as transcribed from the actual tape, went like this:

Yearling sale at Fasig-Tipton, Kentucky, with Ralph Rettler (left) and John Finney (right) on the podium.

Finney: Hip number one-hundred twenty-eight is Ben S. Castleman's dark bay or brown colt, not a bay as your catalogue shows, but a dark bay or brown colt from the first crop of Boldnesian's brilliant son, Bold Reasoning, stakes winner of nearly a hundred ninety thousand dollars, and the first foal of stakes-winning My Charmer, winner of six races and granddaughter of Myrtle Charm, she the dam of Myrtle's Jet from the great family of Myrtlewood.

Retler: Thank y'a, three, four, I'm bid three thousand, four thous'n dollars, let's go boy, at four, four, *five*, I'm bid four-forty five, forty-five anybody, fifty-five, six thous'n then, six then, sixty-five, at seven thous'n, seventy-five, seventy-five, eight then, eight thousand, now nine, ninety-five, ninety-five, now ten anywhere, ten, ten, eleven, I got eleven thousand dollars, eleven-leven-leven-leven . . . *twelve* . . . thirteen, thirteen, fo'teen, fo'teen, fifteen, I'm bid fo'teen, anybody fifteen, Bruce, you're at fifteen, sixteen, sixteen, seventeen, at seventeen, eighteen thousand dollars, you want him at eighteen?, at seventeen-*five,* at seventeen-five, I'm bid seventeen-five, eighteen, eighteen if you want him there, I'm bid seventeen-five, if you want him at eighteen anywhere, at seventeen thousand five-hundred dollars and . . . eighteen you want him, at seventeen-*five* and . . .

Finney: First foal of a stakes-winning dam and by a *runnin'* horse.

Retler: Eight-*teen* if you want him . . . (raps gavel) . . . Bill. Seventeen-five."

As he stepped into the brightly lighted sales ring, the yearling whinnied nervously and tugged at the shank held by a handler.

"Hip number one-hundred twenty-eight," droned John Finney in the litany of the horse auction, "is Ben S. Castleman's dark bay or brown colt . . ."

After the calm of White Horse Acres, this was a strange new experience for My Charmer's son. For two rainy days, he and the other yearlings at the Fasig-Tipton Company's sales paddocks in Lexington, Kentucky, had been inspected by more people than they had ever seen before. Now it was Saturday night, forty-five minutes into the second session of the one-day auction on July 19, 1975. His turn had come.

A patch of adhesive tape on the colt's flank designated his number in the sales catalogue. But the number caused no stir of excitement at the unfinished pavilion alongside the Newtown Pike. As the catalogue showed, the pedigree was adequate but not eye-catching: first foal of a mare who had won only one minor stakes event in two years of racing, and from the first crop of an unproven sire. He was big for his age, well above average, and the color of dark mahogany. But he lacked the sculpted, racy look most buyers favor. He had the kind of unattractive head that horsemen call knotty. And his right front leg toed out, angled outward, a conformational fault that had caused some customers to mark "no" on his page in their catalogues.

Better bloodlines and conformation would have qualified the colt for either Fasig-Tipton's Saratoga Sales in August or the Keeneland Summer Sales opening in Lexington the following Monday. Those are the blue-chip yearling auctions, at which polished sons and daughters of the world's most desirable sires are displayed in manicured stable areas like diamonds at Tiffany's. And the shoppers there aren't looking merely for a horse who can win a claiming race or even an allowance race. They're shooting for the moon, looking for a colt who can win the Kentucky Derby or a filly who can take the Kentucky Oaks. The average amount paid for a yearling at Keeneland that summer would be

$53,637, at Saratoga $37,000. For Mickey and Karen Taylor, now waiting to bid on Hip No. 128, the prices at Keeneland and Saratoga were out of their range.

At Fasig-Tipton Kentucky, in its second year as a kind of "fire sale" preceding Keeneland, the average would be $10,683. As usual, there was talk by the salesmen about "good families" and "black type" (equine ancestors for whom bold-face type in the catalogue indicates stakes successes) and "handsome individuals" deserving careful consideration. But the black type here was less impressive, the sales pitch less flamboyant. What nobody knew then, of course, was that two graduates of the firm's first sale, conducted in a tent the previous year, would account for the Triple Crown in 1976—Bold Forbes ($15,200) winning the Derby and Belmont, and Elocutionist ($15,000) taking the Preakness.

If the international crowd was dressed more casually than for Saratoga or Keeneland, its goal was the same. They were all there: the old wealth and the nouveau riche, aristocrat and hardboot, buyer and kibitzer, brokers with good reputations and kickback hustlers trying to grab a piece of the action by bringing together men with horses to sell and men with the money to buy them. They had been checking the merchandise carefully, looking and listening and scribbling notes in their catalogues. Does this colt toe in when he walks? Is that filly over at the knee? Is the neck too short? From the side, does the hip look long enough to produce the kind of push and power needed by a stakes winner? Crafty trainers had run their hands up and down the legs of baby horses, feeling for hints of future problems. Legs had been bent at the knees, and hooves inspected to make sure a defect hadn't been camouflaged by an irregularly filed shoe. And all the time, the shoppers had been asking themselves: Will the colt with the defiant eyes grow up to be a Kentucky Derby winner? Or will he turn out to be just another bright-eyed failure who eats like a horse but runs like a cow? High-priced failures have always outnumbered the bargain yearlings. Yet Canonero II, the 1971 Kentucky Derby winner, was bought at a yearling auction for $1200. The fascination of racing's most expensive guessing game is that nobody knows for sure.

". . . and the first foal of stakes-winning My Charmer," Finney was saying, "winner of six races and granddaughter of Myrtle Charm . . ."

Dr. Hill with Seattle Slew.

CONFORMATION

Bred for speed, Thoroughbred horses gallop along at nearly forty miles an hour on slender legs that can outrun anything in the animal kingdom. But the legs don't always hold up. A single misstep can end a racing career or a life, as it did in the case of Ruffian. Yet Seattle Slew, a horse with the same kind of blazing speed as Ruffian, remained sound throughout his Triple Crown campaign. And the people closest to him are convinced that it was the colt's dense bone structure that made him less vulnerable to a breakdown than other super-fast horses.

Because of his solid, heavy bones, Slew was able to go through his two-year-old season without developing bucked shins, an inflammation of the cannon bone in the lower leg caused by stress and a common ailment among young racehorses. A horse with bucked shins has to be taken out of training and rested, but Seattle Slew's legs were strong enough to withstand the pressure.

"He's got a very heavy, high quality of bone," says Dr. Jim Hill, the colt's veterinarian and co-owner. "There's a lot of bone there. That's the first thing we look for when we're buying a horse. Before we even look at the overall horse, we have to see what we think is an acceptable set of legs."

Dr. Hill uses the following standards to evaluate a horse's legs: density of bone; proportionate lengths of pastern, cannon bone, and forearm; length of hind leg; angulation of pastern and hock; general conformation of joints. From front to back and from side to side, Seattle Slew's bone density impresses the people who know about such things.

In addition to dense bone, Seattle Slew also has good balance: a well-laid-back shoulder; a relatively long back with strong, close coupling between hip and rib; a long hip with medium angulation; long, heavy muscles rather than bunchy ones; and a good long neck.

"I don't like to see a horse with a head that sticks straight up out of the top of his shoulder," says Dr. Hill. "I like to see a classic length in front with the neck. What you look for is balance, because the head and the neck are used as a balance beam. If you've got a little short stubby neck, or a neck that sets up high, it's hard for the horse to have really good balance."

All of these assets compensated for the fact that Seattle Slew didn't have the handsomest head and that he was "out in the right front," as horsemen say, meaning that his right foreleg toed out slightly. But the good points were not apparent to the bidders who let Slew get out of the sales ring for $17,500. According to eyewitnesses, he was "just another yearling," a horse who passed through unnoticed by most of the crowd.

But Jim Hill was excited by the horse's appearance the first time he saw him being led out of his stall into the muddy paddock at Fasig-Tipton. Hill has never shared the popular opinion of Slew's clumsiness as a colt; to Hill he looked like a runner.

In the horse business, where different judges use different guidelines, there's a saying that the expert is the man who was right once. By that standard, there was no shortage of experts among the five hundred or so potential bidders sitting on folding chairs in the temporary pavilion. Yet only about twenty-five of them had taken more than a brief look at My Charmer's colt during inspection hours.

LeRoy Jolley, an expert many times over, was one of the first to check the colt early Friday morning. Jolley and John L. Greer, one of the owners for whom he trains, didn't look long. It was Jolley who had advised Greer to pay $20,000 at the 1973 Saratoga Yearling Sales for a colt who toed out in both front feet. The bargain purchase, Foolish Pleasure, was voted champion two-year-old, won the 1975 Kentucky Derby, and earned $1.2 million as the most illustrious Saratoga purchase since Man o' War.

"You watch how they handle their feet," Jolley once explained. "You look for a horse with bright eyes and a bold, strong walk. You look and look, and finally they lead one out and there's something that just hits you."

When Paul Mallory led Hip No. 128 out, though, Jolley apparently didn't feel any strong vibrations. He watched the farm manager walk the colt back and forth, said "Thank you," and went on to the next yearling. But now in the sales pavilion, as Fasig-Tipton's president and announcer completed his introduction, the young couple from White Swan, Washington, could feel the tenseness. Like a poker player holding what he considers good paper, Mickey Taylor was trying to look uninterested. But he was ready for action, the kind of action he relished. This was the yearling his friend and partner, Dr. Jim Hill, had put at the top of their most-wanted list. "Mick," the veterinarian had said only a few hours earlier before boarding a New York plane at Blue Grass Airport, "we want that Bold Reasoning colt."

They had bought two yearlings at the afternoon session, for $9700 and $8000, before the thirty-seven-year-old vet flew back to his home in Garden City, Long Island. And earlier in the evening sale, a third yearling had been purchased for $9200. Hill had put a ceiling of $22,000 on the Bold Reasoning colt, knowing his partner would add 10 percent to that figure if necessary. In all, they had looked at more than a hundred of the yearlings, and put prices on eight of them as possible buys.

Their partnership, sealed on a handshake, was suggested by Taylor. He would put up the money, and Dr. Hill would contribute his time, his knowledge, and the selection of the horses. Racing was not their prime objective. The game plan was to buy quick-developing yearlings at bargain prices, get them ready to race, and then sell them early the following season. The original thought was to take the horses to Sunland Park in New Mexico, where two-year-olds can run for first-place purses as high as $140,000 in early stakes events such as the Riley Allison Futurity. If any of the horses on their list could win the Riley Allison, it had to be Hip No. 128. From the first look in the rain Friday morning, when Mallory led the yearling around in mud and water, Jim Hill had talked of balance and bone structure. He had gone back three or four times for further checking.

Now the bidding was starting. Naturally, there was no opening "sledgehammer" gambit, an opening bid of $100,000 or so designed to flatten the opposition. Nor were there any hoarsely shouted calls of "Here!" from sharp-eyed spotters to reflect a bidding war that jumps $10,000 at a time. This was the bargain basement and Ralph Retler, the auctioneer, started the bidding off at $3000.

But for the Taylors, it was a heady feeling. They were only thirty years old, in their second season as horse owners, and here they were, matching wits and money with some of the game's shrewdest traders. It had happened so suddenly, the business success that changed their lives. Before Mickey hit it big in logging, they had more or less been living on Karen's earnings as a stewardess for Northwest Orient Airlines. Now they had money to spare. But their home was still a trailer in White Swan, a town of six hundred people where the only reason they didn't roll up the sidewalks at 7 o'clock every night was that there were no sidewalks. Mickey, a fourth-generation logger, had never had much use for fancy material things. Except money. That, he felt, was how you kept score. Mickey's big score had come in June of 1973, three years after his marriage and a year after he and his younger brother, Quirt, had bought a bankrupt logging company in White Swan for a stake of $500. They had a corner on the pulpwood market when a paper shortage tripled the price of pulp.

Rivals called it luck. With an easy laugh and a reputation for revelry, Mickey Taylor did give some people the impression of a

38

PHYSICAL INSPECTION REPORT
FASIG-TIPTON COMPANY, INC.
NEW YORK • KENTUCKY • CALIFORNIA • FLORIDA
P.O. BOX 36, 40 ELMONT ROAD, ELMONT, N. Y. 11003

DESCRIPTION: NAME _____

1974 dk. b./brn c. Bold Reasoning - My Charmer
YEAR FOALED • COLOR • SEX • SIRE • DAM

OWNER: *Ben Castleman*

INSPECTED AT: *White Horse Acres*

DATE *5-5-75*

ON APPROPRIATE DIAGRAM BELOW, INDICATE ANY PHYSICAL
DEFECT, BLEMISH, OR MAJOR DEVIATION FROM NORMAL
CONFORMATION.

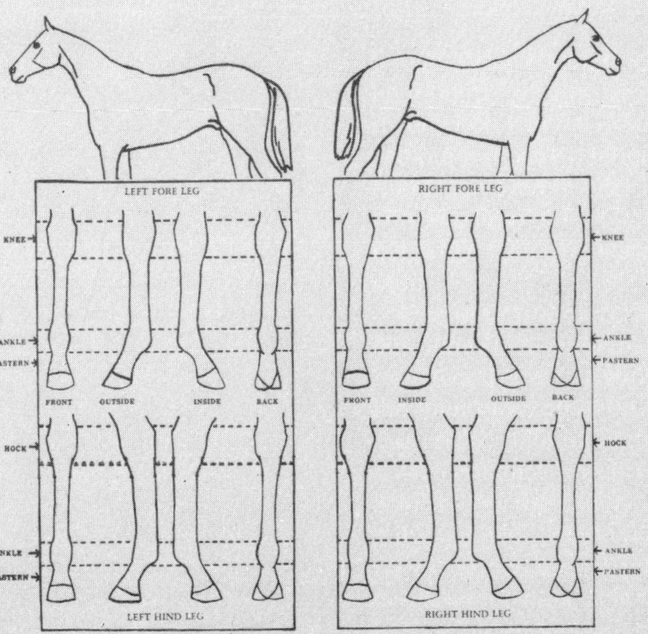

LEFT FORE LEG

KNEE

ANKLE
PASTERN

FRONT   OUTSIDE   INSIDE   BACK

HOCK

ANKLE
PASTERN

LEFT HIND LEG

RIGHT FORE LEG

KNEE

ANKLE
PASTERN

FRONT   INSIDE   OUTSIDE   BACK

HOCK

ANKLE
PASTERN

RIGHT HIND LEG

COMPLETE REVERSE SIDE OF FORM

---

dk. b./brn. c. 2-15

PHYSICAL INSPECTION REPORT   *Bold Reasoning - My Charmer*
CHECK APPROPRIATE COLUMN ON EACH LINE. ANY DEFICIENCY CHECKED MUST BE
ACCOMPANIED BY EXPLANATORY COMMENT.

GENERAL CHARACTERISTICS	Outstanding	Average	Deficient	COMMENTS
CONFORMATION				
SIZE		+		
DEVELOPMENT		+		
BONE AND SUBSTANCE		+		
QUALITY		+		
PHYSICAL CONDITION		+		
APPARENT SOUNDNESS				

CONFORMATION DETAILS				
HEAD		✓		*prominent between eyes*
MOUTH		✓		
EYES		✓		
EARS		✓		
NECK		✓		
SHOULDER	+			*angle good*
BODY				
HEART		✓		
GIRTH		✓		*good back*
LENGTH		✓		
RIB CAGE		✓		
RUMP				
FORELEGS				
FOREARM		✓		
KNEE		✓		*out RF, knee ✓*
CANNON/TENDON		✓		
ANKLE		✓		
PASTERN		✓		
HOOF		✓		
HINDLEGS				
HIP		✓		
STIFLE		✓		
GASKIN		✓		*nice hind leg*
HOCK		✓		*passes close*
CANNON/TENDON		✓		*at hocks*
ANKLE		✓		
PASTERN		✓		
HOOF		✓		
GAIT (AT WALK)		✓		

CHECK AS APPROPRIATE	No	Yes		COMMENTS
MALE WITH UNDESCENDED TESTICLE(S)	✓			
CRIBBER	✓			
STALL WALKER	✓			
WEAVER				

REMARKS *Strong colt. Shoulder developed well, good
angle. Strong back good thru middle, good spring of rib.
Turns out moderately right front from knee down. Quick
appearance*

RATING *75* %.   SIGNATURE *Ted Bates*

RATING: 91-100% OUTSTANDING; 71-90% BETTER THAN AVERAGE; 51-70% AVERAGE; 35-50% POOR;
1-30% UNSUITABLE FOR SALE.

6

wild and lucky Irishman careening through life joking, "Did anyone get the license number of that Jack Daniel's bottle that ran over me?" But beneath the carefree exterior, a second Mickey Taylor existed: shy, level-headed, uncomfortable in anything but cowboy boots and blue jeans, a man with a keen business mind who would confess he had little time for friends because "I work my butt off, and the harder I work, the luckier I get."

For her part, Karen had been keeping an eye on Mickey since they had met on a blind date as high-school seniors. He was from Ellensburg and she lived in Yakima, thirty miles south. Her father and grandfather were both accountants, her mother and grandmother both apple growers. Mickey finally graduated from Western Washington State in 1968, and Karen wound up at the University of Washington.

"My college career," she would explain, "was following Taylor around keeping an eye on him."

Nobody could accuse them of rushing blindly into matrimony. They went together for seven years before being married in 1970 on April Fool's Day (Mickey's decision) by a justice of the peace named Love (Karen's choice). For two years before their marriage and three years after, Karen worked as a stewardess, flying the New York-Anchorage-Tokyo route or dashing off to Hawaii or Miami. Then came the paper shortage, the pulpwood bonanza, and the Taylors began to develop an interest in horses that extended beyond betting on them at Yakima Meadows, Longacres, or tracks in California.

". . . at seventeen-*five*," Retler was saying now. "I'm bid seventeen-five, eighteen, eighteen if you want him . . ."

Mickey, signaling the spotter nearest him with a slight nod of the head, had just raised the bid on the Bold Reasoning colt to $17,500 with a $500 increase. Retler was looking for $18,000, but the action had stalled. Now Finney was trying to revive it with one of his little pep talks. He did not tell the crowd it was "way too cheap" on this one, or that this colt could be "worth almost anything," as he frequently says at Saratoga. But the record shows that Finney did make a brief appeal.

"First foal of a stakes-winning dam," he reminded the bidders in the reverent tone of a preacher promising salvation, "and by a *runnin'* horse."

It was no use. None of the others thought Hip No. 128 was

worth $18,000, and Retler banged his gavel and said, "Bill. Seventeen-five."

Ben Castleman, the breeder, turned to Paul Mallory and said, "Well, he brought more than we were ready to let him go for."

Later, Mickey Taylor phoned Jim Hill in New York and told him they had bought the Bold Reasoning colt for $17,500.

"Super," said the vet.

As far back as late 1973, Hill had advised the Taylors through an intermediary on the purchase of several horses. But they had never met until September of 1974 in Lexington, where the veterinarian and his wife, Sally, were attending the Keeneland Fall Sale. When Hill refused a fee for recommending a yearling that Taylor purchased for $16,000, the young logger told him, "I'll just take the first eight thousand out of any winnings, and then you own half of him." The colt, named Lexington Laugh, would suffer a fatal leg fracture late in 1975 after showing great promise.

The new venture, an expansion of their original deal, was a corporation called Wooden Horse Investments, Inc. Put together by Karen Taylor's father, Delmar Pearson, it was designed to defer income taxes on possible earnings. New York regulations prohibit racetrack vets from having a beneficial interest in a racehorse. Because Jim Hill did not actually own stock in Wooden Horse until June 1, 1977, he felt he was not a horse owner. His wife, Sally, had thought up the name for the venture, working from the fact that Mickey Taylor's money had come from the woods, but not forgetting the connotation of the Trojan Horse, that legendary wooden decoy which had turned things around for the Greeks.

The morning after the Fasig-Tipton sale, Paul Mallory went back to the barn to feed and water Hip No. 128. But the yearling was gone, and the farm manager wondered where his new owners had taken him. The colt hadn't gone far—only a few miles away to a farm owned by the Murty Brothers, air-cargo specialists in horse transportation. Nine more yearlings were bought by Wooden Horse at the Keeneland Fall Sale in early September, bringing the total to thirteen. But only nine stalls were available at the California training center where the Taylors planned to ship their horses. It was decided to keep four of the yearlings in the East, the four who didn't look as if they would be ready in time for the Riley Allison Futurity. One of them was the Bold Reasoning colt. The next stop on his route to the track would be a farm in Maryland.

SCHOOL DAYS

They met in September, the year-old racehorse from Lexington, Kentucky, and the young woman who had grown up in a dream-world of make-believe horses at an orphanage in Lexington, North Carolina.

"Well," said Paula Turner, sticking her hands in the back pockets of her blue jeans, "Baby Huey!"

She said it without any ridicule in her voice. You had to like horses, love them actually, to have spent as much time with them as twenty-seven-year-old Paula Turner had. It was just that this one reminded her of Baby Huey, the overgrown duck in the cartoon strip. He had a big, ungainly body and a big, rough-looking round head and a tiny foal's tail on him that looked ridiculous. That's what set him off the most, she thought, the little tail with its short hairs on such a great big body. He would be a two-year-old in a few months, she realized, and here he was walking around like an enormous baby. She had no idea the official name would eventually be Seattle Slew.

To her, the dark brown colt who had just stepped off the van from Kentucky was Baby Huey. And from the looks of him, she told herself, he would probably take longer to educate than most of the yearlings sent to her for breaking at Andor Farm in Monkton, Maryland. It might be nearly a month, she knew, before she rode him for the first time.

Years earlier, at the orphanage where her grandmother worked and lived, she wouldn't have been able to wait that long. She probably would have tried to ride the colt bareback right away, imagining him to be the Black Stallion of her childhood dreams. There were no real horses in her life then, only the make-believe horses created by Walter Farley's books and her own imagination.

In the second grade, a year before the children normally were taught to read, Paula discovered a book called *The Black Stallion*. She couldn't understand half the words, but she struggled through it, went over it again and again, and learned to read—and to

Paula Turner
holding Slew
for his bath.

Paula with
Walter Farley,
author of
The Black Stallion.

dream. The dreams triggered by the book helped her live with the fact that one of her parents had died, the other didn't stay with her, and home was an orphanage. She would never forget the story: A boy and a horse escape from a shipwreck. . . . Horse saves boy's life by swimming to an island, pulling the boy along with him. . . . They get together. . . . Boy rides horse with no tack, dreams impossible dreams. . . . They get into a famous match race. . . . Nobody except Clocker gives the boy and his horse, called "The Black," any chance. . . . Clocker is the only one who knows. . . . They win the race, pulling it out with a wild, impossible charge.

From then on, Paula began riding horses in her imagination. The closest she got to a real horse was the black-maned mule who pulled the garbage wagon around the orphanage campus. At the risk of being kept indoors a day or two, eight-year-old Paula would ride Mary The Mule as she plodded along. The mule would be the Black Stallion, and they would be in a famous match race competing against the top horses in the world. When the young dreamer finally got a bicycle in the fifth grade, her imagination changed it easily into a horse. The bike became The Black, ready at the touch of a pedal to gallop off and win the famous match race. Until then, Paula herself had been The Black. When the kids played house, making believe they were mother, father, or child, Paula was always the horse: rope in mouth, harness on body, whinnying and tossing her head and pawing the ground with her feet. They called her horse-crazy and nicknamed her Spooky after a real horse that lived on a nearby farm.

When she wasn't playing horse, she was drawing pictures of them. In the sixth grade, riding her bike, she discovered a dark brown mule behind a fence in the woods. She made a halter out of some clothesline and began riding her newest Black Stallion around in his fenced-in area every day after school. One day, riding on a path too close to the barn, she was spotted by the mule's owner.

"Oh, shucks," she thought, "I'm dead."

But the owner was a man who understood. "If you want to ride him," he told her, "just wait till we're through plowing the garden. I'll let you use the bridle."

Thus did Paula Turner begin her formal riding career: on a twenty-year-old mule with his very own bridle and reins, a mule who could be walked and jogged and even taken over small jumps. But that was a long time ago, she thought, and this was business. Her practiced eye told her that Baby Huey, because of his size, might take as much as three times longer to school than her average pupil. She knew it was easy to get carried away with a big, strong-looking horse and think you could do a whole lot with him in a short time. You couldn't. His brain had to catch up with his body. She didn't know too much about this one's background. Just that he was by Bold Reasoning and had been bought at an auction that summer of 1975 by the Taylors, for whom her husband had only recently begun to train. Her job would be to break the colt to the saddle, teach him to respond to voice and hand commands, gain his trust, establish lines of communication that would stay with him the rest of his life.

His schoolyard, leased by the Turners, belonged to a farm of several thousand acres owned by Mrs. Henry Obre. This was fifteen or twenty miles north of Baltimore in Maryland hunt country, a scenic area where rolling fields with post-and-rail fences stretch for miles. The new student's lessons, Paula decided, would begin the following day.

She had plenty of time to devote to him, with only a couple of Milton Ritzenberg's steeplechasers and two of her own three-day-event horses in training at the farm. For the first few days, Huey began learning voice commands such as "Walk" and "Whoa!" while circling his teacher in the stall on a lead shank. Next came the bit and the saddle, and a few more days of circling in the stall, this time on a longe line. Then the classroom moved outdoors into the paddock, where long reins called driving lines were used for the process known as "putting a mouth on a horse." Three weeks later, without having had a rider on his back, Huey had been taught such basic maneuvers as turning left or right in response to the bit, and walking or stopping on command.

To some, the work might have seemed tedious. To Paula Turner, it was second nature. It was probably inevitable that her life would revolve around horses. As a freshman at college in North Carolina, where she played the female lead in the play *Rebel Without a Cause,* she had thought about an acting career. But a girl at school whose horse she rode told her in the spring of their first year that she should be galloping racehorses.

"Do girls do that?" Paula asked.

Hardly any of them did at the time, but nineteen-year-old Paula

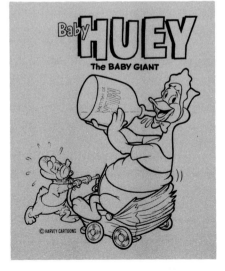

45

became one of the pioneers in racing's feminist breakthrough. By the end of that summer, at tracks in Maryland and Delaware, she was an exercise rider as well as a hot-walker and groom. She had also started dating Billy Turner, a young trainer, who first said he would visit her at college and then said, "We both know I won't, so I guess I ought to marry you."

By now Paula was an experienced horsewoman. In schooling young horses, she tries to have one "argument" with them before sending them to the racetrack, a battle of wills designed to teach the horse to respect and trust the rider's authority. With Huey, the argument came much sooner than she had wanted—the first day she rode him. After a few circles in the paddock, he just planted his feet and refused to budge. Nothing she did could get him going. But she knew she couldn't walk away from it. If she did, the horse would know he was boss. At the racetrack, he could become a cheater or a rogue, and everybody would lose.

The argument lasted several minutes. She finally had to whack him repeatedly on the rump with a riding crop, hard enough to raise welts, before he moved forward. When he did, she patted him on the neck and soothed him. From that first step, he did everything his rider asked—but not in a subservient manner. She knew she had never lost his confidence, only gained his respect. She had always believed that horses can sense the thoughts and feelings of their riders. Huey had compromised, and he was still fearless. He didn't just walk, he marched. Jogging in a large field filled with what Paula calls "monsters," he didn't even glance at the strange sights most young horses spook at: a stone wall from an old jump course, sitting all by itself in the middle of the field; a salt lick for cattle; a dead tree on its side near a stream bed.

Baby Huey in his paddock at Andor Farm in Maryland.

"This is an unusual horse, Billy," she told her husband on the phone. "Very determined. I can't believe how businesslike he is."

Eventually, before she sent him to Belmont Park in February, Paula was jogging Huey as much as three miles a day. She would see him later at Belmont a few times, and gallop him at Saratoga the next summer. And on a September afternoon in 1976, a year after he arrived at the farm, she would get a phone call there from the Taylors and Hills in New York. They had just seen the colt make his racing debut.

"Congratulations," Karen Taylor would say to her, "for breaking a very good horse."

CHOW

Fast as he is, Seattle Slew costs no more to feed than any other racehorse with a healthy appetite. Without eating like a glutton, the average racehorse can put away nine or ten quarts of oats a day. Add some hay, some sweetfeed, and a carrot or two, and a horse's daily feed bill at Belmont Park can climb to six dollars, double what it was a few years ago. And that doesn't count vitamins.

Like most other working Americans, Slew has a light breakfast, a moderate lunch, and a big supper, though the hours are different. Breakfast, put into his feed tub by the night watchman soon after 4 o'clock in the morning, consists of two quarts of oats. At lunchtime, around 10 a.m., it's two or three quarts of oats and half a dozen carrots. Supper, usually served around 4 o'clock in the afternoon except on the day of a race, is the major feed of the day: six quarts of oats, two quarts of sweetfeed (a mixture of corn, oats, dried molasses), and another half-dozen carrots sliced up in the mixture. John Polston, the colt's groom, feeds him lunch and supper. Polston says Slew doesn't "talk" before mealtime the way some horses do, nickering and whinnying when they hear the stablehands getting chow ready.

"All he ever does," the groom confides, "is sometimes jump around in the stall and raise hell when it's feeding time."

Every feed is laced with powdered vitamins or vitamin pellets. Slew never has to ask for hay or water. He always has some of both in the stall, with one exception: race day, when the hay is removed and kept off the menu entirely unless the star boarder gets fidgety. The hay is left on the floor of the stall rather than in a rack. Says Billy Turner: "A hayrack is just one more thing a horse can hurt himself fooling around with."

Sugar is not part of the colt's menu, even as a special treat. But he loves Jordan almonds, the candy-covered kind you buy in movie theaters. And he knows he can always count on Paula Turner, his trainer's wife, for an almond or two. As for the carrots, Billy Turner's reasoning is simple: "If they're good for people, why wouldn't they be good for horses?"

Mike Kennedy and Slew.

DEBUT OF A CHAMPION

There was nothing in the *Daily Racing Form* of September 20, 1976, to suggest anything out of the ordinary. No comment about a well-bred newcomer or a promising maiden or a horse with fast works. Just the simple, noncommittal line: "Begins career today."

The past-performance data for the first-time starter in the fifth race showed three ordinary workouts. Nothing to get excited about. But high above the stands at Belmont Park, in the rooftop pressbox, the Squirrel was humming to himself in a "nobody here but us chickens" tone. This was the mystery horse he had been waiting for since Saratoga, the two-year-old colt he had twice seen Billy Turner trying to flag down because he was going too fast. After the second workout at the Spa, which he happened to see while having a late breakfast on the clubhouse porch, he had told the trainer he would "find out who that sucker is." Now he could see it in the *Racing Form*: Seattle Slew, dark bay or brown colt by Bold Reasoning out of My Charmer, trained by William H. Turner, Jr.

Turner hadn't run him on closing day at Saratoga, the Squirrel knew, because the horse had hurt his leg in the stall. It didn't matter. A few hours from now, he would be making his racing debut in a six-furlong sprint for two-year-old maidens. And the Squirrel was dreaming about a lot more than peanuts. The program odds on Seattle Slew were 10 to 1, and none of the six *Racing Form* selectors had picked him.

In the stands below, early birds in a Monday crowd of 18,745 were lining up at the daily-double windows. Other horseplayers wandered with open *Racing Form*s in front of them, poring over the past performances as raptly as pilgrims reading the Scriptures on their way to a favored shrine. It was 12:30 p.m., an hour before post time for the first race. And during racing's Happy Hour, the fresh-start wait before a new card begins, nothing is impossible. All the losers from yesterday have been scrubbed off

Mike Kennedy
and Billy Turner
head back to
the barn after
a dawn gallop.

the pari-mutuel blackboard. Now every race shapes up as a wedding, not as a funeral.

"Whaddya hear?" the horseplayers called out to their friends, searching for scraps of information. "Who d'ya like?"

There was talk of this horse or that horse owing somebody money, talk of the shipper just vanned in from out of state, talk of jockey changes and drop-downs and blinkers being added. But there was hardly any talk about the horse in the fifth race named Seattle Slew. Bettors looking that far ahead could see from their programs that he was the "eight" horse in a twelve-horse field, was owned by Karen L. Taylor, would be ridden by Jean Cruguet, and, like all the others, would carry 122 pounds. In a racing-silk rainbow with so many reds, greens, and whites, his colors would at least be easy to follow: black, yellow yoke, yellow hoops on sleeves, and a yellow cap with black pompon.

Additional information in the *Racing Form* was skimpy. The August 11 grass workout at Saratoga, erroneously reported at 1:00 2/5 instead of 58 2/5 and credited to "Seattle Sue," had somehow become 1:02. And the only other works listed, both half-mile breezes on a sloppy track at Belmont, were nothing to write home about: 48 seconds on September 11 and 48 1/5 on September 17.

The ups
and downs
of a horseplayer.

For some reason, either because the clockers missed it or because they had stashed it, there was no mention of the 1:10 1/5 for six furlongs at Saratoga.

All this pleased Mike Kennedy, now preparing to take his place behind an exacta window in the Belmont Terrace dining area on the fourth floor of the clubhouse. In his afternoon role as pari-mutuel clerk, Kennedy would be selling exacta tickets and, on the final race, triples. In his morning role as Seattle Slew's exercise rider, he had known for a long time what the colt could do. Kennedy's spirits already matched the sparkling 78-degree Indian Summer weather. This was the day he and Huey were going to kill the country. None of the tip sheets, he knew, even mentioned the horse. He had checked it out. So the mutuel should be $16 at least, a 7-1 payoff, and that would make it a happy day. He had given a pocketful of money to a friend to bet for him, provided the odds weren't too low.

Kennedy wondered if the word might be getting out. Already, on the way in, people who knew he worked for Billy Turner had stopped him to ask about the first-time starter.

"Well, I don't know," he had told them without enthusiasm. "He's got some ability. But there's a lot of nice maidens in there."

51

There were, too: the field was packed with high-priced promise that included well-bred colts by such respected sires as Graustark, Never Bend, Damascus, In Reality, and First Landing, among others. Kennedy knew that Reggie Cornell, a shrewd trainer, was high on a first-time starter named Winaben, a gray colt who had been breaking stopwatches in morning workouts. But the exercise rider also knew that nobody was going to beat Huey. No other horse in the world could do three-quarters in ten and one the way he had done. If anybody else had been hiding a fast one in their barn, he was going to be disappointed. When the starters loaded Huey into the gate, they would be lighting the fuse on half a ton of nitro.

Yet Kennedy wondered why there weren't more tips on the horse going around. It was almost too quiet for comfort, like the eye of a storm. There were too many touts and hustlers on the racetrack, all of them playing the game of O.P.M.—Other People's Money. The worst of them were the tout-service syndicates, the easy-buck hustlers whose mailing-list gulls were nothing more than sitting ducks. Had one of the services, he wondered, notified its clients that it had been "given the green light" to release exclusive word on a "guaranteed New York winner" that happened to be Huey? Kennedy knew the game. He had seen enough of the ads in gaudy handicapping papers, invitations that began: "Would you pay $15 for a Guaranteed Long Shot Winner going at a New York track within the next 10 days? This horse must positively win or we shall refund your money at once. Need we say more?"

The touts couldn't lose, of course. If the horse won, the money stayed in the bank. If it lost, free tips on other horses could be offered to soothe and tease the clients. At the very worst, a few refunds might have to be made.

Then there was the ultra-confidential approach, one that made Kennedy more uncomfortable: "I have been sworn to absolute secrecy, but I must classify this longshot sleeper as the strongest, most powerful betting tool of the year! No one knows a thing about him." Had the tout services found out about Huey? Probably not, he convinced himself. They usually just picked out horses that were coming into form and let the law of averages do the rest. Kennedy dismissed the thought of a tout-syndicate coup from his mind. The horses were at the post for the first race. In a few minutes, he would begin selling exacta tickets.

Outside the clubhouse, in a lot where trainers, jockeys, and track officials park, Billy Turner stopped to talk to an old black man in a golf cap and T-shirt who was splashing soapy detergent from a plastic bucket onto the front fenders of a Cadillac. Like so many others, the man they called Carwash was a permanent part of the racing mosaic: a seventy-two-year-old horseplayer who had been washing cars at New York tracks for more than thirty years, working mornings in the stable area and afternoons outside the clubhouse. His real name, unknown to most racetrackers, was John Gorham.

"He's got a chance," Turner was saying now, and the old man nodded his thanks.

The first race was over, sending horseplayers who weren't alive in the double back to the drawing board. On the second floor of the clubhouse, John Esposito had already turned the pages of his *Racing Form* to the fifth race. He was smiling as he read Sweep's analysis: "CARIBERT comes out of a maiden race from which Catalan and Western Wind have rebounded with strong efforts. The promising Steve DiMauro trainee was shut off trying to split horses in that event when beaten only a length, but should leave the maiden ranks today. WINABEN comes to the races off some fast works (1:11 3/5, 34 4/5, 1:00 1/5 in the slop) and could be tough at first asking. PRINCE ANDREW is bred to be a good one."

Billy Turner had been a regular at Esposito's Tavern, across the street from the Belmont Park stable area, since the days nearly twenty years ago when he was a steeplechase jockey. He had never stopped dropping in even after he became a full-fledged trainer. He called it "my office." John Esposito, forty-seven, oldest of the three brothers who ran the place, had known about Huey since early July. Late one afternoon, Turner had invited him over to the barn.

"What do you think of this guy?" the trainer had said, pointing to a big, nearly black colt.

"Billy," the bartender had said, "this horse reminds me of walking through the barns in the old days and looking at all those Bull Lea colts Ben Jones used to have for Calumet. Big, raw-boned horses. Muscular-looking horses."

"Can run," he remembered the trainer saying. "A steamroller. It's Huey. You'll get his real name when he runs."

And sure enough, there it was right in the program: Seattle Slew.

If the name was new to Esposito and most other people, it was
no surprise to the two couples now watching the races from Milton
Ritzenberg's clubhouse box: the Taylors and the Hills. They had
submitted the name to the Jockey Club for approval nearly a year
earlier, an application signed by Karen Taylor and specifying
Wooden Horse Investments, Inc., as the owner of the horse. Karen's husband, Mickey, and her father, Delmar Pearson, were
listed as the stockholders in Wooden Horse. To all but a few
insiders, though, Seattle Slew belonged to Karen, a former airline
stewardess. Mickey would not come into the ownership picture
publicly until the following winter. And it would be May of 1977,
after the Kentucky Derby, before Dr. Jim Hill and his wife, Sally,
would emerge as co-owners of the horse with the Taylors. But
when they talked about the colt on the day of his debut, they talked
as they had from the beginning about "our champion."

The name reflected the dual ownership: Seattle for the Taylor
territory, Slew for the swampy, alligator-filled sloughs or "slews"
in the South Florida area where Jim Hill grew up. As Karen would

explain, "We wanted a snappy name, and 'White Swan Slew' just didn't sound right." The Jockey Club, national registrar for the identification and naming of all Thoroughbreds in North America, received the name application in November of 1975. It was approved the following January, and the tag was mailed on January 21, 1976.

On the day of Seattle Slew's debut, it was unlikely that the members of the Eastern racing establishment, sitting in nearby boxes, regarded the newcomers in Ritzenberg's box as any kind of competitive threat. They were just two attractive young couples having fun at the races and waiting to watch a first-time starter who was 10-1 on the morning line. But Mickey Taylor, a two-fisted gambler in his younger and wilder days, wouldn't be betting a dime on Seattle Slew. Once, before he hit it big in the logging business, Mickey won $62,000 on an 80-1 shot at a California track. But since 1973, when he started buying horses, he had given up betting on them.

As far as the public knew, Jim Hill was just the vet who looked after Seattle Slew's health, and Sally Hill was the vet's wife. But Wooden Horse was thriving. The previous week, at the Keeneland Fall Sales, in Lexington, Kentucky, Mickey and Jim had made a bid of $75,000, three times their normal yearling-sale maximum, in an effort to land Seattle Slew's half-brother. But the yearling colt by Jacinto, foaled by My Charmer at White Horse Acres in 1975, had gone to Jack Gaver of Greentree Stable for $100,000. Now they were waiting for the debut of that colt's big brother, back in shape after wrenching a hock at Saratoga. The mishap had delayed his timetable about a month.

While they waited for Seattle Slew, the Taylors and Hills talked about Forego. The big gelding, shooting for his third straight title as Horse of the Year, had won the $173,200 Woodward two days earlier with 135 pounds on his back, setting a stakes record of 1:45 4/5 in the mile-and-an-eighth handicap. Some horse, they all agreed.

The fourth race was official, and the opening odds for the fifth race had gone up on the tote board. As the Taylors and Hills filed out of the box, on their way to the paddock, the off-track money wagered on the race at two hundred OTB (Off-Track Betting) shops in the New York area flashed onto the board. The new odds made them all blink. Their 10-1 long shot was the 7-5 favorite.

Seattle Slew
coasting home
an easy winner
in his first race,
September 20, 1976.

55

"I hope the bettors are right," said Mickey Taylor.

Upstairs at his Belmont Terrace exacta window, Mike Kennedy fought an impulse to cry. Here he was with his hard-earned money, ready to kill the country, and all of a sudden . . . bang. Nearly $30,000 on Huey, all from OTB. The whole thing was weird. It must have been the clockers, he thought, or the amateur bookies. The bookies must have given the secret to their clients. He knew it wasn't Billy Turner's money, because twenty dollars was a big bet for Turner. It had to be the clients.

Now the whole place was buzzing. People were gathering around Kennedy's window like moths around a light bulb, trying to get his attention: "Hey, Mike, what's going on about this horse of yours? How come you didn't tell us about him?"

"Well, he's got some ability," the exercise rider said, trying to pull himself together, "but there's some nice maidens in there and . . ."

He knew the words had a hollow ring. And when the friend who was going to bet for him came by and asked about the odds, he told him to forget it. You couldn't bet Huey now, not at those odds, and Kennedy had a feeling it would be that way from now on.

Turner's stablehands were in or around the paddock out behind the stands when the odds board there showed the 7-5 flash on Huey .

"Who told?" Sam said, shaking her head. "Oh, well, I only wanted to see him run, anyway."

The whole stable had been psyched up to watch and to bet—if Huey didn't go off at 2-5 or something like that. Mainly, they wanted to see him run: John Polston, his groom; Donald Carroll, the hot-walker; Donald's brother, Dennis, the young assistant trainer; and Sam and some of the other grooms and exercise riders.

"Put your riders up," the paddock judge called out, and trainers, cupping hands under the bent knees of jockeys, boosted the riders into the saddle.

Huey, prancing now with Cruguet on his back in the black and yellow silks, circled the walking ring and marched out past the bronze statue of Secretariat toward the track. On the tote board, his odds had gradually begun to lengthen, first to 8-5, then 9-5, then 2-1. The name Seattle Slew hadn't appeared on any of the licensed tip sheets sold at the track for a dollar or more. The Beard

Seattle Slew's second victory— the $11,000 added Black Pool at Belmont, October 5, 1976.

and The Centaur both had Caribert, a gelded son of Roi Dagobert, as their best bet of the day. Clocker Lawton, Clocker Rowe, New York Handicap, and Powell also had Caribert on top. Proud Arion was Top Turf's "most preferred" play of the day, and Jack's Little Green Card liked Winaben. The odds on Seattle Slew went to 5-2, still favoritism, as the horses were loaded into the starting gate on the distant backstretch of the mile-and-a-half track.

"He broke bad," said Dennis Carroll, providing a commentary for the stablehands as he watched the horses through binoculars. But then, a few moments later, saying it as calmly as he could: "Now he's on the lead."

It was just what they had expected. A million things can go wrong in a horse's first race, and only one thing can go right: he can win. Huey, the tenth horse to come out of the gate, just put his head in the air and ran and kept running and just laughed at them all, as if to say, "Wow, this is easy!" He won by five lengths in 1:10 1/5, the same time he had worked in at Saratoga a month earlier.

On the way back to the barn, Mickey Taylor and Jim Hill were stopped by a trainer who had seen the race. He wanted to buy the horse for $100,000. Three days later, the same trainer would raise the bid to $300,000, and Jim Hill would tell him, "That's a good offer, but Mickey doesn't need the money."

For Billy Turner and his stablehands, there was only one place to celebrate Huey's first victory. They adjourned to Esposito's, a first-aid station where plastic parrots roost above the bar, where wall posters remind patrons that "horses need love, too," and where regulars frequently introduce their friends with the warning: "I like the guy, but he's got no class." Huey's first payday wasn't much: $5400 from a gross purse of $9000. He still wasn't completely smooth but the natural ability was there.

"Huey's just a great big kid who thinks it's all a game," said Turner, waving to John Esposito for a round of drinks.

"Hey, we won a race," said Sam, ordering a White Russian instead of her usual Coke.

Mike Kennedy arrived, explaining that he hadn't bet a nickel. If he had known Huey would go to 5-2, he said, he would have bet. The Squirrel came in later, confessing he had "told a few people," including his delicatessen man, about the Bold Reasoning colt.

"When the custodian of the pressbox finds out," Turner announced, ordering a drink, "you know you're in trouble."

As the pay phones kept ringing with calls from Saratoga friends, asking how the horse made out, some of the details began emerging. The clockers, it was said, had bet their own money for the first time in years. Smart-money gamblers had tried to bury their action at off-track shops in Connecticut, figuring the payoff would be bigger in that state's separate-pool operation on New York races. It wasn't. The payoff in Connecticut was $5.40 for $2, the exacta of Seattle Slew and second-place Proud Arion $57. At the track, the win payoff was $7.20, the exacta $63.40. But the troops at Espo's weren't concerned now with pari-mutuel prices. Nobody said it, but they all knew that this horse could be worth a lot more than a winning bet. They were thinking now of the Champagne Stakes, the country's oldest race for two-year-olds, coming up at Belmont in less than a month.

At a table in the corner, Billy Turner was telling Frank Tours, a backstretch liaison man for the New York Racing Association, that For the Moment looked like a logical Champagne favorite. The colt trained by LeRoy Jolley had won three straight races, including the Belmont Futurity nine days earlier. But Tours, leaning across the table, was disagreeing with his friend.

"Forget about For the Moment," he said, lowering his voice. "Turner, this horse of yours may *never* get beat. Now don't mess it up."

The first stage of the rocket had ignited, lifting Seattle Slew off the launching pad. The next two stages, a seven-furlong allowance race won on October 5 and the $137,250 Champagne Stakes on October 16, would send him into orbit as America's champion two-year-old.

But a hitch six days before the Champagne came close to wrecking the mission. Jim Hill sensed trouble the minute he saw Billy Turner come out of the barn rubbing his hands together. Hill knows a lot about Turner, enough to have recommended him to the Taylors as a trainer. One of the things he knows is that when Turner rubs his hands together, he's got something on his mind. And the horse was supposed to have his final serious workout that morning for the Champagne.

"Anything wrong?"

"Jim," came the reply, "we got a little something to look at."

Inside Barn 60, Seattle Slew was taking stiff, uncomfortable steps. Both rear legs were swollen, or "filled," as horsemen say, in the area of the ankles. The vet's immediate thought was that something really bad had happened, like pulled suspensories. But a closer inspection disclosed the cause of the trouble: two small open sores, one on each pastern.

"It looks like a superficial infection," said Hill. "I think we can nip it if we get right on it."

Wearing bandages, Seattle Slew went out on schedule for his dawn workout. Afterwards, the sores on his legs were treated with surgical soap and healing ointment. Then he began receiving injections of antibiotics and Butazolidin, the anti-inflammatory medication permitted in New York for training purposes but not for racing. Under the rules, the medication would have to end before Friday, when entries for the Champagne would be taken. By Tuesday morning, the soreness had disappeared and the swell-was subsiding. Treatment with the antibiotics and "bute," as the drug is called around the racetrack, continued through Thursday. Though the infection would not be cleared up entirely for six weeks, the problem had been solved. And Huey, now known publicly as Seattle Slew, was ready to astound the racing world.

He was wound so tight that Mike Kennedy, the day before the race, needed all his strength and guile to pull the colt up after a three-furlong blowout in 34 1/5 seconds.

Yet some of the public selectors put For the Moment at the top of their line. He was already a million-dollar colt, a half-interest in him having been sold the previous month for $500,000. Since taking the Belmont Futurity, he had added a division of the Cowdin Stakes to his list of victories. Others in the ten-horse field for the Champagne included Ali Oop, winner of the Sapling Stakes; Turn of Coin, with triumphs in the Tremont and Sanford; Sail to Rome, winner of the other division of the Cowdin; Sanhedrin, and Western Wind.

In contrast to his more seasoned rivals, Seattle Slew went into the 105th running of the Champagne with only two starts behind him: the six-furlong debut and the seven-furlong allowance event for nonwinners of two, a test he had won by 3½ lengths as a 2-5 favorite. But the tip-sheet selectors had learned their lesson. This time, on the day of the Champagne, nearly all of them had Seattle Slew on top. Most of them made him their best bet.

Billy Turner was terrified, but not about the opposition. It was the No. 3 post position that worried him. He was afraid that if Huey got off slowly and was trapped along the rail, he might run right over the top of the other horses. But Huey didn't have to. Favored at 13-10 by the crowd at Belmont Park, he opened a daylight lead before the field had gone a quarter of a mile. When For the Moment challenged him in the upper stretch, he laughed at his million-dollar rival and pulled away to win by 9¾ lengths with the fastest mile ever run by a two-year-old: 1:34 2/5. And at the finish, Jean Cruguet was easing him up in what a *Daily Racing Form* chartwriter called "an easy score." In one blazing twenty-six-day span, the colt who began the season as Baby Huey had brought off a tour de force unmatched in American racing.

After his second race, the colt's owners had raised the insurance on him from $50,000 to $250,000. Now they increased it to $2 million. But a tougher decision remained: Should he be sent to Maryland to run in the Laurel Futurity? Or should he be taken out of training and rested for 1977?

"Do we want to make bucks?" Mickey Taylor and Jim Hill asked each other. "Or do we want to have a real good three-year-old next season?"

Slew winning
the Champagne,
October 16, 1976.

Six days after the Champagne, they reached their verdict: stop. Both felt confident that the Champagne had wrapped up an Eclipse Award for their colt. They were right. There was disagreement among the voters, with Run Dusty Run and Royal Ski getting good support. Each of those colts had raced nine times. Run Dusty Run had won six races and finished second twice, while Royal Ski's record showed six firsts, a second, and a third. But Seattle Slew pulled the most votes, and Smiley Adams was outraged.

"Seattle Who?" the pelican-jawed trainer of Run Dusty Run bellowed after the ballots were counted. "It don't matter how easy he did it, he only had three races. It's not right."

But Seattle Slew's backers asked the question: "Which horse would you rather have in your barn getting ready for a Triple Crown campaign?" At Esposito's, anyway, the answer was never in doubt.

61

DERBY DAY

Suddenly, it was the first Saturday of May. In his stall at Churchill Downs, a dark brown colt who had been sleeping on his side scrambled to his feet and nudged the empty feed tub.

"All right now, Hugo," his groom said, "get yourself together. Breakfast's on the way."

It was 4 a.m. in Louisville, dark and drizzly and humid. Before the day was out, the three-year-old horse known to the world as Seattle Slew would be going to the post as a strong favorite in the 103rd running of the Kentucky Derby. As the sportswriters put it, he was still undefeated, untied, and unscored upon—an easy winner in all six of his races since he made his debut the previous September at Belmont Park.

John Polston poured two quarts of oats laced with powdered vitamins into the feed tub, then sliced up a few carrots for dessert. But the horse would get no more than a few flakes of hay today, and then only if he became restless. Breakfast normally would have been served by Mickey Taylor's sixty-three-year-old father, Chester, who had the night watch on Derby Eve. But the colt's groom, living in the tack room at Barn 42, couldn't sleep. He woke up at 3:30 and told Chester to go and get some sleep in the camper where he was staying with his wife, Leola, near the stall.

They were two of the nicest people he had ever met, Polston thought: quiet, pleasant, always the same every day. Having Chester around since Florida as chief watchman, and Leola as housemother and cook, had been a big help to the stablehands.

While the groom tended to the horse, Billy Turner had already taken the prescribed breakfast for trainers of Derby favorites: an antacid tablet. At 4:30, Turner was knocking on Mike Kennedy's door in the Executive Inn, a few miles from the track, and calling softly, "Mike? Are you up?" The exercise rider had left a wake-up call for 5 o'clock, but he was already wide awake. The Taylors and Hills, occupying adjoining rooms nearby, would be getting up

Donald Carroll holding Slew after a dawn gallop on Derby Day. Donald has an especially close relationship with this horse. In fact, he considers Slew his best friend, and the feeling seems to be mutual.

Eddie Arcaro with Billy.

soon. Only Jean Cruguet, the jockey, would be getting a little extra sleep. He had volunteered to go to the track early, but Turner told him to stay in bed. Cruguet was the one member of the team the trainer wanted well rested for his work with Seattle Slew.

The headlines in the morning papers for May 7, 1977, now being delivered, reflected the colt's status as the people's choice. In Lexington, sixty-five miles to the east, where the once-awkward hero was born at White Horse Acres, the front-page salute in the *Herald and Leader* proclaimed: "It's Slew's Day!" The *Louisville Courier-Journal* heralded the return to Kentucky of the home-state celebrity with an eight-column banner across the front page that read: "Can He or Can't He? Slew Will Say Today."

The stories beneath the headlines told the familiar details: how the colt purchased for $17,500 as a yearling became the two-year-old champion on the strength of just three races; how he broke a track record at Hialeah in his debut as a three-year-old, then won the Flamingo Stakes and Wood Memorial; how he had never gone to the post as anything but a betting favorite, the highest odds on him being 5-2 in his first start; how a victory today would make him only the fourth undefeated horse to win the Derby.

But the stories raised questions, too. With only six races and two workouts of three-quarters of a mile or more under his saddle, had he been undertrained for so demanding a test? Would he self-destruct if some other horse forced him into too fast an early pace? Was he just coasting in the Flamingo and the Wood, or was he getting tired? What about Run Dusty Run and For the Moment, two of his most formidable rivals? In twenty-six starts, their combined record showed twenty-four firsts and seconds.

The skeptics were still insisting that Seattle Slew lacked the foundation to go the Derby distance of a mile and a quarter, still accusing him of being an overrated fraud, still waiting for him to lose so they could say "I told you so."

"He's had everything his own way so far," Smiley Adams, the colorful, crewcut trainer of Run Dusty Run, was quoted as saying. "He can be beat."

From Jimmy Jones, the man who trained Citation for his Triple Crown sweep in 1948, came the diplomatic comment, "You wonder if he's finishing as well as he should be." And Eddie Arcaro,

The morning
of Derby Day

Derby post
parade

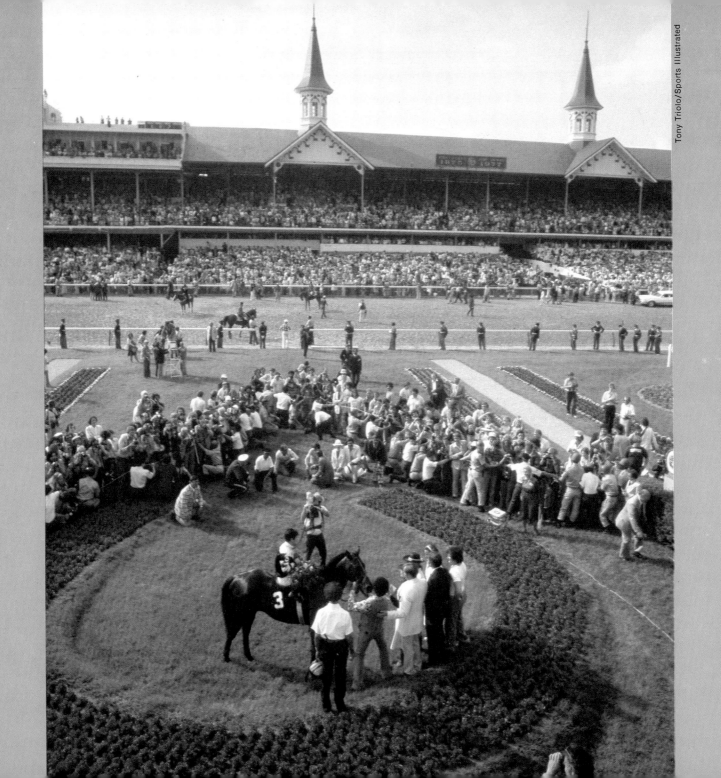

the famous ex-jockey who rode five Derby winners, including Citation and another Triple Crown champion, Whirlaway, was making it known he wasn't overly impressed with either Seattle Slew or Cruguet. Arcaro would be doing the Derby television commentary for the American Broadcasting Company with Howard Cosell.

Driving to the track in the dark, Turner and Kennedy couldn't help thinking about the day in Saratoga nine months earlier when the snoopers started asking about a Bold Reasoning colt who supposedly had worked six furlongs in 1:10 1/5. Now everybody knew about Huey. As they drove through the pre-dawn showers, they talked about the second-guessing that had been going on over the horse's light training program. It had been a hectic ten days since Seattle Slew arrived in Louisville on a cargo plane from New York. No other horse race in the world gets the week-long attention the Derby gets, and hundreds of columnists, reporters, and sportscasters had descended on the scene.

It wasn't so much the constant questioning that bothered Turner. With his patience and sense of humor, he knew how to handle the press. When each new arrival asked why he called the stable pony Steamboat, for example, it was easy to answer, "If you rode him, you'd know why." But Turner found it impossible to answer the knocks about his training methods, the criticism that he was not training his horse hard enough for a race like the Derby. When Seattle Slew worked a lazy mile in 1:41 1/5 the previous Sunday, horsemen shook their heads and wondered why the trainer hadn't ordered something faster. But Turner knew this was a difficult horse to work, a colt who would do something sensational if you asked him for speed when all you wanted was a reasonable workout. All along, the trainer's goal had been to bring his horse into the Derby as fresh as he dared.

But Thursday was a disaster. To compensate for the slow Sunday work, Turner planned to give Seattle Slew a fast drill of four or five furlongs on Thursday. But a fierce early-morning rainstorm, what the natives call a "frog strangler," turned the track into a muddy swamp, rutting it with gullies in certain places and leaving ridges in others. A gallop in those conditions, the trainer and the exercise rider agreed, would be asking for trouble. So with Kennedy on his back, Seattle Slew merely walked: first in the

Howard Cosell with Karen.

backstretch, while sheets of lightning flew across the sky; then to the paddock, to escape the storm; then back to a starting gate on the backstretch; and finally back to the barn.

"What are they going to do?" the hardboots brayed. "*Walk* that sonofabitch to the Derby?"

That left only Friday, the day before the race, for the necessary workout. Because the Derby was so close, it had to be cut to a three-furlong blowout, the fast pre-race tuneup that horses need to clear their lungs, much as a car's carburetor is cleared by a brief burst of speed. With the track back in good shape, Seattle Slew went in 34 2/5 seconds. Turner started breathing almost normally. Now there was nothing much anybody could do except cross his fingers. If a Kentucky Derby candidate isn't ready by dawn on the first Saturday of May, the day when America's most famous race is always held, he'll never be ready. Since the race is only for three-year-olds, a horse gets only one chance to win.

By the time Turner and Kennedy reached the barn, Polston had already put the tack on Seattle Slew. Jim Hill arrived a few minutes later. Around 6 a.m., with Kennedy on his back and a stable pony accompanying him, the colt went for an easy one-mile gallop that would help him relax. Then Polston washed him down, and Donald Carroll, the hot-walker, led him around the shed row for half an hour. David Pierce, Slew's blacksmith, was standing by in case a shoe needed changing. Returned to his quarters by 7:30, the Derby favorite turned his head toward the rear of the stall and began to doze standing up.

Even now, young people who had spent the night on lawns or sidewalks near Churchill Downs were beginning to line up at the entrances to the track. The gates would open in half an hour, and the collegians in search of a happening would file into the track to stake out choice viewing points in the infield or to set up their blankets, beer coolers, and picnic baskets. After record attendances all week, there had been speculation that the eventual crowd might be larger than any other except the turnout of 163,628 at the 100th Derby in 1974. But the damp weather so early in the day was expected to persuade at least some customers in neighboring states to stay home and watch the race on television.

At 9:30, Jean Cruguet and his wife, Denise, returned to their room at the Executive Inn after a leisurely breakfast. The jockey had eaten lightly: a poached egg on English muffin, prune juice, black coffee with artificial sweetener, and a vitamin pill dutifully offered by his wife. Except for a few cups of coffee in the jockey room, he would take nothing more until after the Derby. It was not a question of weight, an occupational hazard for most jockeys. It was a question of comfort. When he eats too much, Cruguet tends to become lazy. And today was no day to feel lazy.

Later on, he would nap for an hour and a half. Then he and Denise would drive to the track with Mike Kennedy at 2 p.m., a ten-minute ride that would stretch to half an hour because of the Derby traffic. And he would tell his wife to meet him after the race at the place where the victory parties were held. But now, in the quiet of his room, it was time to savor his new role as one of the country's most fashionable jockeys. Cruguet inserted a cigarette into a filtered holder that was supposed to make him stop smoking, and stretched out on the bed to read the *Racing Form* and the morning papers he had bought in the lobby. He noted with satisfaction that the fifteen-horse field would produce a Derby purse of $267,200, of which the winner would get $214,700. Good, he thought, mentally computing the traditional jockey's cut of 10 percent. Purses like that would help keep Cruguet and his family (wife, nine-year-old daughter, Leslie, and mother-in-law) living in style on their elegant six-acre estate in Brookville, Long Island, where pheasants came out of the woods to stroll on wide expanses of rolling lawns. Denise had found the place the previous August, about the time his luck seemed to turn.

There had been so many bad breaks, the thirty-seven-year-old Frenchman thought, since he came to the United States in 1965 after interrupting his riding career with three years in the French Army and a brief fling as a boxer. There was Hoist the Flag, the brilliant three-year-old he hoped to win the Derby with in 1971 until the colt fractured a leg in a workout. There was San San, a year later in France, winning the world-famous Arc de Triomphe with another jockey ten days after Cruguet broke both hands in a spill. Even last December, in Florida, it looked as if the bad luck was still with him—a shoulder separation in a spill at Calder that knocked him out of action for six weeks.

But Oliver Cutshaw, his agent, stayed close to the Seattle Slew camp, and when the shoulder healed, Cruguet was still Slew's

Billy Turner
fielding questions
during Derby Week.

Oliver Cutshaw,
Cruguet's agent.

75

rider. Cruguet respected Cutshaw, a former jockey and trainer, as a thorough horseman, who had done him a considerable favor in 1966, helping him get started as a jockey in this country by putting him on all the horses Cutshaw was then training in Maryland. Cutshaw's new role as Cruguet's agent, an association formed the previous summer at Saratoga, had worked out well. Cruguet's mounts in 1976 earned $1,800,000, and only $94,350 of that came from Seattle Slew.

Yes, thought Cruguet, his luck was changing. What difference did it make if he was only five feet three inches tall? He had become one of the biggest men in racing. It didn't bother him any more that French horseplayers sometimes used to call him "*Mains de Fer*," meaning Iron Hands; or that most people, even friends, pronounced his first name "Gene" instead of the right way; or that certain trainers had been telling the Seattle Slew people they had the world's worst bum for a rider; or even that a New York trainer's pre-Derby insult had received national publicity: "Two minutes is a long time for the Frenchman to go without making a mistake." Let them have their little joke, the Frenchman thought as he relaxed on the bed and smoked his cigarette. Jean Cruguet had the best three-year-old in the country, maybe in the world. And before sundown, everyone would know it.

While Cruguet relaxed in luxury, John Polston lowered himself into a lounge chair outside the tack room at the track and prepared to take a nap. The groom covered his face with his stable hat, the blue denim sunhat he had worn at Seattle Slew's first three races and still carried tucked into his belt whenever the colt ran. Hugo won with it, he knew. Listening to the music from a stable radio, Polston thought of all the ways the horse had changed his life: the winter in Florida away from his wife and two growing boys, an absence his wife, Ola, had opposed; no more partying till 2 or 3 o'clock in the morning with the guys or even going out much with Ola. There was too much responsibility at the barn for that— getting to bed early because he wanted to be at his best when he went into the horse's stall in the morning.

But maybe it was all going to pay off. There would be bonuses, and Billy Turner and the Taylors were good about that. It wasn't easy bringing up a family on a groom's take-home pay of $145 a week, even when your wife worked. The rent for the apartment in Queens was $250 a month, and then you had your food and all the

Slew with part of his crew, Jim Hill and Billy Turner (upper right) and Mickey and Karen Taylor (lower right).

76

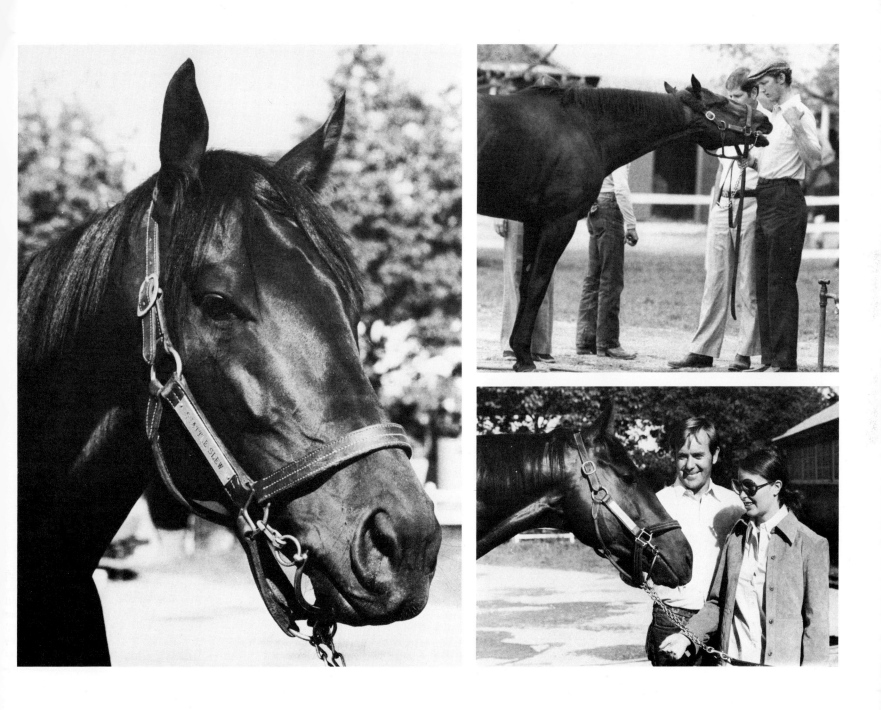

Turner and
Cruguet
in conference
just before the
running of the
Wood Memoria
at Aqueduct,
April 23, 1977.

other bills. He wasn't even gambling much any more, because he didn't want to jinx the horse. As Polston began to doze, he was awakened by clicking noises. A television crew was taking his picture, and asking now for an interview. Politely, he told them no. He'd rather have generosity than publicity.

At 11:30, just in time to carry the first race, two Louisville television stations began their live Derby Day coverage. They would go nonstop until 5, when the network would take over. Even now, despite an occasional sprinkle of rain, the infield was a crowded blue-jean carnival: Frisbees, volleyball games, picnics on the grass, beer-drinking, socializing, young women in halter tops being tossed into the air on blankets by college youths wearing T-shirts with messages like "So Many Girls and So Little Time." Eventually, the crowd at the track would grow to 124,038, fourth largest in Derby history. Over in the grandstand, a vendor predicted he would sell five twelve-drink trays of $2.50 mint juleps in the forty minutes before the Derby. "Everybody wants to be able to go home," he said, "and tell their friends, 'I was sipping a julep and watching the Derby.'"

At the Executive Inn, the Taylors and Hills had the television sets in their adjoining rooms tuned to different channels and were shuttling back and forth between the rooms to catch all the Derby Day action. They had ordered bacon, lettuce, and tomato sandwiches from room service. To the public, Karen Taylor was still the owner of Seattle Slew, though her husband, Mickey, had by now become an equal partner in the daily interviews. Jim and Sally Hill were still virtually anonymous; he was the horse's veterinarian, the man who spotted Seattle Slew's potential as a yearling, and she was the vet's wife.

In Florida the previous winter, a reporter had asked Dr. Hill what was wrong with the horse that required the constant presence of a veterinarian. "It's not what's wrong with him," Hill had replied. "It's what's right with him." Nobody had made anything of the remark at the time. But now, as they had from the beginning, the two young couples talked of "our champion." And their champion was favored to fulfill a dream many millionaire horse owners spend a lifetime pursuing. C. V. Whitney, for example, had been trying for nearly half a century to win the Derby. Yet only a few days earlier, Whitney had withdrawn his latest Derby contender, Coined Silver, after a disappointing prep race. In only their fourth full season of racing, the Taylors had the big horse.

Early in the week, Mickey Taylor had said, "I'm a logger and Karen's an ex-airline stewardess. What more is there to say?" But the press had found more to say. Much more. By now, most of America knew the script: the love story of an all-state basketball star (Mickey) and a future airline stewardess (Karen) from different small towns in Washington who met on a blind date as high-school seniors. Everyone now knew that they went together for seven years before they got married, and that Mickey, a fourth-generation logger, had hit it big by buying pulpwood low and selling high; and that their home was still a trailer in White Swan, Washington, a logging town of six hundred people, two gas stations, a luncheonette open only at lunchtime, four churches and a diner that closed at 8 o'clock every night, all of it in the middle of the 800,000-acre Yakima Indian reservation in the foothills of the Cascade Mountains.

All week long, Karen had charmed the media with a cheerful style that seemed equally at home with television, women's magazines, and *The Blood-Horse* and the *Thoroughbred Record.* Commenting on the fact that she had turned thirty-two in February but her husband wouldn't be thirty-two until June, she confided, "He used to tell me I might be older, but that he was wiser. Now he says I robbed the cradle." If she seemed overly deferential to her husband, it was by design. When she wanted attention, she said, she called him "Mouse."

Although he bragged that "mass confusion is our best policy," Mickey Taylor and his brother-in-law, Delmar (Butch) Pearson, had organized the Derby logistics well. Nearly a hundred relatives, friends, and loggers—employees from White Swan—had been put up downtown at the riverfront Galt House as guests of the Taylors. When the Taylors and Hills left for the track around 2 p.m., Mickey would be thinking of the difference a year could make. Last year, sitting on some apple boxes, he and his father had watched the Derby on a television set in the stable area of Sunland Park, a minor-league track in New Mexico across the line from El Paso, Texas. This year would be a little different.

Out at Churchill Downs, at Barn 42, the hours crept by. Even Lance, the Doberman who helps guard Seattle Slew, appeared restless. Around 3:30, with the countdown entering its final stages, the Derby favorite showed how concerned he was. He stretched out on his side in the stall and fell sound asleep.

In a bar near the stable area, Billy Turner nursed a vodka tonic and thought of flamingos. Hialeah Park. Color it pink. That's where it began, of course, back in January before they knew for sure whether the horse in Barn D was the same one they had had in 1976.

Toward the end of the month, the Taylors and Hills flew to Miami after a Caribbean sailing vacation. They saw Mike Kennedy, on a leave of absence from his New York pari-mutuel job, ride Seattle Slew in his first strong gallop of the winter. A little entourage followed the horse to the track on a route taken by so many Derby hopefuls over the years: along a sandy path in the Hialeah stable area between rows of towering Australian pines; through the paddock, with its royal palms and its life-size statue of Citation in a pool of water lilies; past Mediterranean stairways that curved down out of stands covered with purple bougainvillaea blossoms; and finally out front, where flamingos rose from their infield lakes to glide, elongated in flight, like pink paper airplanes.

"That's him," the exercise rider said when he brought the colt off the track. "He's back."

Now they were having a drink on the first Saturday of May, Turner and Mickey Taylor and Jim Hill, waiting to take the horse over for the Derby. The trainer thought of Huey stretched out on his side in the stall, sound asleep. Just like a good fighter before a big bout, able to doze right off. Under different circumstances, Turner might have worried. Maybe the colt didn't feel well. Maybe he had a fever. But they had been through that in Florida.

An hour before Huey made his first start as a three-year-old, on March 9 at Hialeah, he stood around looking listless and then just lay down and fell asleep with his head on the floor of the stall. Turner remembered taking big strides and rubbing his hands together, the way he does when he's concerned, and telling Dr. Hill, "We'd better take this horse's temperature, Jim, he could be sick. What if he did this an hour before the Derby?"

So they checked the temperature, and found it normal. And Huey walked out onto the track and ran the fastest seven furlongs in the fifty-two-year history of Hialeah. For raw speed, it had to be one of the most awesome displays ever seen on an American racetrack. The horse had been away from the races for nearly five months. He was coming back against an undefeated colt named White Rammer, a three-year-old sprinter with nothing but "1's" in his past-performance chart at every call of every race. And Huey ran him into the ground.

It was unreal. They went the first quarter in 22 1/5 seconds, head to head, with the rider on White Rammer slapping and banging and Cruguet just sitting still. They were still heads apart going into the turn. Then Huey shook loose with a half in 44 flat, bent double. He was gone. At the eighth pole, he had run six furlongs in 1:08, faster than any horse in the history of Hialeah. He just galloped home from there, his ears pricked like a saddle horse out for a leisurely canter. Cruguet hadn't touched him once, yet the final time of 1:20 3/5 was less than a second short of the world record for seven furlongs. Turner remembered the comment in the *Racing Form* chart, a rare tribute that began: "Seattle Slew, in a remarkable performance, took charge from along the inside in the backstretch . . ."

White Rammer hung on for second place, nine lengths back. But he didn't eat for three days. Just stood in his stall with his head down. That was the worst thing that could happen to a good horse, Turner had always thought: to run as hard as he could against a superior horse. It took a lot out of him, mentally as well as physically.

Cruguet had looked back over his shoulder two or three times, and Mickey Taylor had joked after the race, "We're going to have to get Jean a rear-view mirror for Christmas." That was after Cruguet returned to the jockey room and yelled at Lazaro Samuell, rider of White Rammer, for the early cowboy tactics that got both horses stirred up.

"You knew you had no chance," he snapped. "Nobody was gonna catch this horse today."

"Not even in a patrol car," Mickey Solomone, the rider of one of the also-rans, had chimed in.

Talking to the press, Turner called it an "unbelievable" performance. But it really hadn't surprised him that much. He had trained the colt to run fast the first time out, and to win. Turner

Cruguet and Seattle Slew running away from the others in the Flamingo at Hialeah, March 26, 1977.

82

Slew takes
the lead early
in the Wood
. . . and keeps it.

SLEW'S HEADPIECE

Apart from speed, one of Seattle Slew's most prominent trademarks has been the distinctive headpiece he wears when he goes to the track for a gallop or a race. It did not become part of his tack until he began his Triple Crown campaign as a three-year-old in Florida.

The apparatus, shaped like an inverted Y and known by the brand name of Sure-Win, is designed to keep a horse's tongue under the bit by holding the bit well up (or back) in the mouth. Horses breathe through their noses, but they run with their mouths open. If a horse gets his tongue over the bit, the rider cannot control him since the bit is out of place. Some trainers use a tongue-tie, a strip of cloth wrapped over the bit and tongue and looped under the horse's chin, to keep the proper alignment.

Made of rubber, the orange-colored bit holder worn by Seattle Slew attaches to the bridle in one piece. Because of its design and construction, it is extremely flexible, stretching easily under pressure.

When Seattle Slew went to Saratoga as a two-year-old, he was using a plain snaffle bit. But after two fast workouts there, it was decided he was getting so strong that a ring bit would have to be used. He wore the regular ring bit, designed to give a rider more control, in his three races as a two-year-old at Belmont Park. But he got his tongue over the bit moments before going into the starting gate for the Champagne Stakes, and an assistant starter, reacting alertly, had to reach over and slip the tongue back underneath. When Seattle Slew started galloping in Florida the following winter, it was decided to switch to the headpiece that has appeared in photographs ever since.

wanted him to come back feeling like a two-year-old, running with an attitude of "Boy, is this fun." And he had. When Huey arrived in Florida on December 27, after two months of doing nothing in New York, he spent the first month or so at Hialeah just galloping. The real workouts began in February, workouts so quick he ran faster than the track record for five furlongs in one of them.

Sally and Jim Hill join the Taylors, Cruguet, and a member of the Wood family for the trophy presentation after the Wood.

Huey had been a lot of horse in Florida, Turner knew, an awful lot of horse. People didn't realize how strong he was. On the way to the track one day, when Steamboat kept nipping at him, he just reached out and grabbed the stable pony on the side of the neck and lifted him right off the ground. Another day, Lou Rondinello had pointed at a good-looking colt and asked Turner, "Do you know this horse? It's the horse that Seattle slew." It was Sanhedrin, badly beaten in the Champagne. Both Rondinello and LeRoy Jolley, the trainer of For the Moment, had ducked Seattle Slew in Florida. But they were both here at Churchill Downs now.

And their horses could be tough, Turner thought, especially For the Moment. He was more aggressive since LeRoy put blinkers on him, and he was coming into the Derby off a big effort in the Blue Grass Stakes. Anything could happen, the trainer knew. Any horse could lose, as Native Dancer, Secretariat, and even Man o' War had proved. They said that Native Dancer, with an undefeated record of 11-0, couldn't lose the 1953 Derby. But he did, after getting bumped on the first turn. You had to worry, too, about how your horse acted in the paddock and the starting gate. Either one could beat you. But the Florida campaign, he thought, had been good experience for Huey .

For a while, the Royal Ski balloons had been a conversation piece. The name of that colt, one of the rivals Seattle Slew beat out for the Eclipse Award, appeared on one side of the balloons. The opposite side carried the putdown "Seattle Who?" But the promotion didn't bother Turner. He knew what he had in his barn. And Royal Ski, before long, went sour, sulking in his stall and refusing to extend himself on the racetrack.

A basic battle plan for Seattle Slew had been formed by his owners during their two-week sailing vacation on a sloop skippered by Jim Hill and stocked with a cargo of steaks, gin, suntan lotion—and dreams. The colt would have three races before the Derby: a prep race at Hialeah, then either the Flamingo Stakes there or a shorter race in New York, and finally the Wood Memorial.

Before the prep race, called the Flamingo Hopeful, the Taylors and Hills decided to hedge their bets a little. They tried to sell a one-fourth interest in the horse, talking to four different people. But after he broke the track record, Seattle Slew was taken off the market and his insurance was raised from $2 million to $3.5 million. The new premiums were $2000 a week.

A consensus then was reached that the Flamingo, at a mile and an eighth, made more sense than a shorter race in New York, where the colt would have to run hard all the way. The $139,000 Flamingo at Hialeah on March 26 fit the schedule perfectly. And it turned out to be as easy as they had expected. Huey went right to the front, opened a fifteen-length lead between calls on the final bend, and coasted home four lengths ahead in 1:47 2/5, the third-fastest time in the forty-eight-year history of the race. But the skeptics, including Eddie Arcaro on national television, weren't overly impressed. They argued that Seattle Slew had tired badly in the final eighth of a mile and that Cruguet had lost his cool by moving with the horse too soon.

Turner, though, knew the jockey had simply followed orders. Cruguet had been told to keep the colt busy on the last turn, because Seattle Slew frequently was pulled up at that point after morning workouts so he could leave the track through a gap near the quarter pole. When Cruguet chirped to him through the final turn, he just took off.

When he came north to his home base at Belmont Park on the last day of March, Huey found a red carpet waiting. Instead of being sent to Barn 60 with the rest of the horses Turner trained, he was assigned by the New York Racing Association to the still-vacant barn used in warmer weather by the Greentree Stable of John Hay (Jock) Whitney.

"They must think a lot of this horse," Turner remembered John Polston saying. "*Nobody* ever uses the Greentree stalls."

Eventually, Huey and his stablemates were given new quarters at Barn 54, a more secluded site with its own walking ring and grazing area. The stable had moved up the ladder, and the once-klutzy Huey had taken it there. But the 53rd running of the $110,300 Wood on April 23, over a tiring track after a month layoff, turned out to be a hard race. The colt won it handily, though the margin of 3¼ lengths over fast-closing Sanhedrin was the narrowest of his career. But the time for the mile and an eighth was a comparatively slow 1:49 3/5, and Seattle Slew was blowing when Cruguet pulled him up after the race. He had never done that before.

"Take your bankroll to Kentucky," one of his heavier-betting critics announced gleefully. "This horse can be had."

In the *Racing Form*, a poll of trainers produced a headline that read "Many Are Impressed by Slew's Wood, Few Are Scared." What the critics didn't know was that Turner had backed off on his colt's training for eight or ten days after the Flamingo, and again when Clev Er Tell, a dangerous rival, was knocked out of the Wood by a leg injury. Getting a horse ready for the Derby, he felt, was a little like serving a crêpe suzette: you had to get it out of the pan and onto the table at just the right moment.

Seattle Slew, the trainer thought as they ordered another drink, probably hadn't really been ready for the Wood. But he was ready for the Derby. Turner knew it.

A BLANKET OF ROSES

Finally, a voice on the stable-area loudspeakers: "Attention, horsemen. Bring your horses to the paddock for the eighth race."

The waiting has ended. In a little while, the outriders will be coming over to organize the fifteen-horse procession for the 103rd Kentucky Derby. After all the speculative oratory of Derby Week, the time has come to let the horses do the talking.

As soon as Seattle Slew steps onto the track on his way to the paddock and hears the crowd, he begins to react. John Polston feels the colt's neck muscles tighten as he pushes harder against the halter and shank.

"Easy, boy, easy, Hugo," the groom says, trying to reassure him. "Gonna be real light today, just a little workout is all. You the best."

The horse's entourage keeps pace with him, handlers accompanying a heavyweight champion to ringside: Billy Turner, his trainer; Mike Kennedy, his exercise rider; Mickey Taylor and Jim Hill, the co-owners; and a squad of security men. A dozen or more photographers and reporters trail along behind. Cindy Hostettler, a free-lance pony girl recommended to Turner by a friend, rides alongside Seattle Slew on a tall cow pony with a braided mane. When someone asks if she has ever taken a Derby winner to the post, she smiles and says, "No, this will be the first time."

Turner's usual hunt-meet tweed cap and turtleneck jersey have been replaced by a formal suit, starched white shirt, and necktie. It is barely 5 p.m., too early, he and some of the other trainers feel, to take the horses over for a race that wouldn't start for forty minutes. On a hot and humid day like this, a horse can lose the race in the paddock. While the rest of the procession stays fairly close to the outer rail of the clubhouse turn, Seattle Slew is escorted by design down the center of the track away from spectators who might reach out and try to touch him.

In the jockey quarters behind the stands, Jean Cruguet lounges in front of a television set. For Seattle Slew's rider, with no other

Cruguet trying to settle Slew on their way to the post.

91

mounts on the card, the time has passed slowly: half an hour in the steam room, more for muscle toning than to take off weight; then the whirlpool, a cold shower, and a massage, part of his daily routine; later a visit from Eddie Arcaro, who calls him a good jockey, apologizes for knocking his ride in the Flamingo and says, "I hope you win the Derby"; an interview with a television crew from Argentina; some shoptalk with colleagues who have ridden in earlier races and tell him the inside part of the track is good. Now, as he watches Arcaro and Howard Cosell on national television, Cruguet wonders why the former jockey is knocking his horse.

Near the passageway that leads under the stands to the paddock, Seattle Slew begins to prance as the band suddenly strikes up the national anthem. He is up on his toes, dancing from side to side. A film of sweat appears on the gleaming dark-brown flanks. The colt is starting to break out, to become "washy," as horsemen say, a pre-race condition that no trainer likes to see. Turner, apprehensive, goes up to help Polston hold the horse steady as they move through the passageway and on into the paddock. The enclosed paddock, hot and crowded, is a circus of wall-to-wall people. A mob of shouting, banner-waving spectators surround the area, pressing against the wire screens and hollering, "Hey, Slew!" Their hero's eyes flash, and he lashes out with a hind leg that thuds into the wooden side of the open stall. Sweat runs down his neck and sides, dripping from his belly as if a faucet had been turned on.

"This guy is feeling very bad, Johnny," Kennedy says to Polston. "He's not shaking, though. That'd really blow his mind."

Some of the other three-year-old colts, especially For the Moment, are becoming a little washy, too. But Run Dusty Run, the main challenger, stands quietly looking at the spectators beyond the screen. He has had fourteen races, and he has become something of an old pro. Seattle Slew, the most lightly raced horse in the field, has had only six. He has never washed out like this before.

"Easy, Huey," Kennedy keeps saying as Turner puts the saddle on. Polston, in the middle, needs all his strength to hold the colt. The groom's flowered shirt and vest, part of a three-piece "Derby suit" he bought at a discount for seventy-five dollars after Slew won the Wood Memorial, are wet with perspiration. He is glad now he didn't wear the jacket, glad he decided just before they came over that it would be too dressy for a groom whose work never ends.

The minutes drag by. Mickey Taylor and Jim Hill, trying to keep people away from the stall, worry about the amount of fluid their horse seems to be losing. Karen Taylor and Sally Hill share the apprehension as they stand in the center of the sweltering paddock, wondering why it's taking so long. John Fulton, the young trainer of Steve's Friend, the Hollywood Derby winner owned by George Steinbrenner, sees the wrung-out favorite and thinks: If we're ever going to beat him, maybe this is the day; he may beat himself.

Upstairs in the nearby jockey room, a voice says, "Riders for the eighth race, let's go." Down the stairway and into the paddock come the jockeys, the peacocks of the racing world. Like airline pilots, jockeys are never supposed to look concerned. So Cruguet, dismayed by what he sees, merely smiles and nods professionally as the others in the Slew Crew greet him. Inside, he feels nothing but clammy despair.

His horse, the jockey fears, is falling down, coming apart. How can he run a true race when he is washing out so badly? But then Cruguet, too, sees that Seattle Slew is not trembling. There is hope. If the horse were shaking, the jockey knows, it would mean his nerves were gone, and all would be lost. But he is not trembling. He is not afraid. As jockey and trainer talk, they remind each other of this.

"Bill," Cruguet says, "I try to settle him down as soon as I get on him."

Twenty minutes after the horses enter the paddock, the signal goes out to put the riders up. As Turner boosts Cruguet into the saddle, he repeats an earlier directive: "Remember, Jean, keep him busy from the quarter pole home. Keep flicking that stick, even if you're fifty in front. This is the Derby."

The Taylors and Hills head for their second-floor boxes, but traffic slows them. They will not get there for ten minutes, only a few minutes before the horses are loaded into the starting gate and long after the playing of "My Old Kentucky Home." But Seattle Slew, third in line, hears the Derby theme song as he steps onto the track, and it stirs him up even more. The pony girl has to hold his bridle.

93

"Look at him, Howard," Arcaro is saying on national television. "He's washed out. That's a very bad sign."

Cruguet pats his horse on the neck, ignoring the music. The first time he heard "My Old Kentucky Home," when he rode an 18-1 shot in his first Derby six years earlier, the song did something for him. He thought the people sang for him because he was on a horse, and it made him feel like a big man. But in his third Derby, on a horse favored at 1 to 2, he is concentrating more on business than on sentiment. He takes Seattle Slew over onto the backstretch, walking him, jogging him, getting him away from all the people and the other horses. He doesn't want any riders coming alongside and chirping to get his mount worked up. He talks to the horse and whistles softly, trying to block out the crowd noise around him, and the horse pricks his ears and listens to his jockey.

Now the drama begins to unfold quickly. The riders walk or jog their horses back toward the starting gate, actually two gates linked together, at the head of the long stretch. The crowd becomes quieter. Other sports spectaculars can drag on for hours, days, even weeks. The Derby, the race they call the "most exciting two minutes in sports," says it all in a hurry. From the public-address system comes the familiar alert, a tense moment at any horse race but always something special before this one: "The horses are at the post."

Cruguet will be going into the gate early, because horses are put there in order of post position. Though Seattle Slew wears No. 3 on his saddlecloth, he will be in the fourth post position. His jockey considers the alignment perfect: slow-breaking horses on the inside, Sanhedrin and Sir Sir; another sluggish beginner, Get the Axe, with Shoemaker on him, to his immediate right, and a horse with good early speed, Bob's Dusty, to his immediate left. As a peace-setting rabbit for Run Dusty Run, his stablemate, Bob's Dusty, will come out of the gate running, and probably drop over to the rail. It couldn't be better, Cruguet feels.

The horses are coming up behind the gate. Only a few more seconds. Suddenly the pony girl, Cindy, blurts out, "Kiss me for good luck." Cruguet, surprised by the timing, gallantly prepares to deliver a brotherly kiss on the cheek. Before he can, Cindy leans over excitedly, grabs hold of the jockey, and kisses him on the mouth. But he recovers his composure quickly as a gateman takes hold of Seattle Slew to lead him into the padded stall.

"Don't grab him in the gate," the rider tells the assistant starter. "Just pat him, take a very light hold, because he get up and fight you if you grab him."

Seattle Slew stands quietly as the other horses are loaded into the gate. A split second after the last horse goes in, the favorite turns his head to the right in the narrow stall. As he does—"They're Off!" The starter has pushed the button, and the doors of the gate have banged open. Seattle Slew comes out high and sideways, like a crab, veering to his right as the gateman tries to push him out of the stall. He is at least two or three lengths behind his rivals, outbroken by everything else in the field. And as the jockeys on the outside horses bring their mounts in a little toward the rail, a solid wall of hooves forms in front of him.

Paula Turner, watching with Karen Taylor's parents, the Pearsons, sees the rest of the field come out and thinks: Oh, God, Huey's still in the gate. . . . For Mike Kennedy, standing with his wife, Denise Cruguet, and Milton Ritzenberg, the immediate concern is that the colt will try to run right over the horses in front of him. . . . And in Elmont, Long Island, at a friend's apartment where she has gone to avoid the crowd at Esposito's, Sam stares at the television screen and thinks: What an unlikely way to lose the Derby.

"Seattle Slew broke slowly," comes the ominous explanation from the announcer. But Jean Cruguet can't hear him. All he hears is the crowd, a noise like that of walls falling down, erupting the moment the gate opens. He sees all the other horses in front of him. Slightly off balance, he fights to bring Seattle Slew back in toward the rail, back to the race. As he neck-reins his mount to the left, Cruguet tilts sideways, but he is in control of the horse. His jockey's mind has already asked the question: Do you take back or do you go? Play it by ear. The ear, what does she say? It must be a split-second decision, more reflex and instinct than deliberation.

He sees Bob's Dusty, ahead and to the left, moving out fast to challenge for the lead. The rabbit's jockey, he sees, is doing what the trainer told him to do. If he stays where he is, Cruguet thinks, I am stuck, he can bury me, I go nowhere. But he is sending his horse. Cruguet sees the opening and makes his decision. He turns Seattle Slew loose. The black and yellow silks spring for-

95

ward. They bound past Sanhedrin, follow Bob's Dusty through traffic, force their way between Sir Sir and two horses to the right, Flag Officer and Affiliate. Within an eighth of a mile, Seattle Slew rushes at For the Moment, in the lead on the rail now after being steered there from an outside post position by Angel Cordero. Bob's Dusty has drifted to the outside, and his rider is trying to bring him back in to trap the favorite. But Cruguet has too much horse now. He wheels Seattle Slew to the outside, clearing For the Moment's heels and brushing Bob's Dusty as he pushes his way past.

At the gold-topped finish pole the first time around, a quarter of a mile from the start, Seattle Slew has caught For the Moment. They are racing head to head. For the Moment has run the first quarter in 23 seconds; allowing a fifth of a second for each length lost coming out of the gate sideways, Seattle Slew has drawn even by running the first quarter in 22 2/5 or less. They have a mile to go.

Paula Turner can't believe what has happened. It is the wildest run she has ever seen any horse make, something straight out of *The Black Stallion*.

Cruguet knows you don't ask for racing room in the Derby, the way you can in normal races if you're in trouble. In the Derby, you have to make your own luck. And he and his horse, he tells himself, have just done it. They are out of trouble. Now he concentrates on Cordero. It was Cordero, Cruguet feels, who won the 1976 Derby, not Bold Forbes. And he suspects that the Puerto Rican jockey intends to try the same strategy today: take command of the track, fight off anyone who wants to challenge him, put the pressure on, make the other horse quit. All right, let's make sure. Cruguet tries for the lead, sees Cordero resisting him, and decides not to use Seattle Slew too much at this point. They are both running fast enough.

They race together into the first turn, For the Moment on the inside, Seattle Slew on the outside. Cruguet understands Cordero's plan: hook this horse who has always had things his own way, go head to head with him, put pressure on him. They curve into the backstretch, reaching the half-mile in 45 4/5 seconds. Until Bold Forbes set an identical pace, no horse had ever run that

Getting off to a bad start. Slew is second from left; the two horses nearest the rail are not visible in this shot.

fast that early in a Derby and still finished in the money. But Seattle Slew's fractional time, considering the bad start, has to be more like 45 1/5. The speed duel has carried them far ahead of the others: four lengths ahead of third-place Bob's Dusty, the outclassed rabbit; nine lengths ahead of fourth-place Run Dusty Run; twelve lengths ahead of fifth-place Sir Sir; nearly twenty lengths ahead of tenth-place Sanhedrin.

After three-quarters of a mile, reached in 1:10 3/5, Cruguet has eased Seattle Slew off the pace, a length back. But when the announcer calls "For the Moment on top, Seattle Slew second by four," some of the Slew Crew members whose view is blocked think mistakenly their horse has fallen four lengths behind. He hasn't. Cruguet has had a steady hold on him all the way down the backstretch, because he doesn't want to give him the bit too soon. At the three-eighths pole, midway through the final turn, the Frenchman decides it is time to go. Time to ask his horse to run, to extend himself. Time to go past Cordero. Cruguet's hands have been restraining Seattle Slew, keeping him from self-destructing with a suicidal pace. Now he pushes forward with the reins, putting pressure on his mount's neck. Go ahead, horse, do what you want.

The black and yellow silks surge forward. They pull up alongside the orange and black worn by Cordero. Glancing to his left, Cruguet sees For the Moment in distress. His head is low, the Frenchman thinks, very low, and Cordero he just pump, pump, pump, but nothing come up, the well is dry. Cruguet knows that Cordero could make trouble for him by carrying Seattle Slew wide, the same thing he did in last year's Derby to For the Moment's full brother, Honest Pleasure. But the Puerto Rican jockey is staying on the rail, riding straight, and Cruguet thinks: That's nice, Angel, you got class; you tried your best and now you know you're beat, and you respect this horse of mine enough so you don't want to see him get beat any other way. As they come to the quarter pole, at the head of the long stretch where the race began 1 minute 36 seconds earlier, Cruguet gives himself another order: Don't just stay alongside. That can give a tired horse courage to keep going. You got to go by him and then it's over, you get him completely. It's like a prizefight, you got to knock your opponent down.

Now, at the quarter pole, Cruguet asks his horse to do even

more. He raps him on the flank with the whip, and Seattle Slew begins to draw away. When he changes leads in the upper stretch, going from a left-foot lead to a right-foot lead on his stride, Cruguet raps him two or three more times. When a horse switches leads, the jockey knows, he can sense he will be asked to run, asked to give a little more. Seattle Slew widens his lead to two lengths, then three as For the Moment begins to fade and Run Dusty Run charges into second place with an eighth of a mile to go.

Denise Cruguet, watching her husband, wants to shout but can't. When she gets excited, she tends to be very quiet. Now she grabs Milton Ritzenberg's arm and silently begins to squeeze. She will continue to "squeeze, squeeze, squeeze," as she explains later, until the race is over.

As Cruguet goes past the eighth pole, only 220 yards from the finish, he knows he is going to win. He hears only the noise of the crowd, a wave of sound that drowns out everything. But out of the corner of his eye, to the right on the outside, he sees gold and red silks. He knows it is Run Dusty Run, the only rival he feared, and he does not want to take any chances. Not in the Derby. He taps Slew three or four more times. With a hundred yards left, Cruguet just goes with the motion of his horse. There is no need any more to ask for extra speed. Everyone in a position to see knows by now that Seattle Slew is going to win the 103rd Kentucky Derby.

The others gain a little, but Slew goes under the wire nearly two lengths in front. Cruguet takes a strong, steady hold on the reins and starts pulling him up, letting him know it's over. But when other horses catch up and go past him on the clubhouse turn, Slew tugs against the bit again, wanting to run. He is so willing, so courageous, Cruguet thinks as he brings his horse to a stop in the backstretch and lets him stand for a few moments to catch his breath.

Now the dross of Derby Week hoopla has been burned away by competitive reality. What remains is racing's favorite rite of spring: another Derby winner, cantering back alone to be draped with a blanket of roses against a backdrop of twin spires. When the winner is undefeated, as only Seattle Slew and three others have been, the impact is even greater.

Seattle Slew begins drawing away from For the Moment (8) in the upper stretch. Sanhedrin (2) is now in eighth place and Run Dusty Run (1A) is third.

Yet even as Slew canters back, his critics are downgrading his effort. They have seen what they wanted to see: the unbeaten wonder horse in trouble, getting dirt kicked in his face for the first time, being jostled and bumped, fighting for his life. And some of them remain unconvinced.

"He *still* doesn't have the figure," bellows one pressbox handicapper.

"He won't win the Belmont," promises another.

"Only the best of an ordinary lot," Arcaro tells the national television audience, citing the unspectacular time of 2:02 1/5 but saying little or nothing about the atrocious start or the brutally fast early pace.

For the Moment, the rival in that speed duel, has finished eighth. Velasquez, the rider of third-place Sanhedrin, claims foul against McHargue, the jockey on second-place Run Dusty Run, for alleged interference near the finish. The stewards disallow it.

Photographers swarm around Seattle Slew. With his groom holding him on one side and the Taylors on the other, the Derby winner marches into the horseshoe-shaped enclosure in the Churchill Downs infield to get his blanket of roses.

Billy Turner, superstitious about winner's-circle appearances, stands off to the side. He has watched the race on a closed-circuit television set in the grandstand, and now he tells reporters: "He was challenged, and he met the challenge. That's the most thrilling thing to me. And he overcame adversity."

As guards fight to control the crowd behind a rope barricade, a young man in a white T-shirt slips through with the official party. He has the beefy look of a college football tackle, and Jim Hill hears him say pleasantly, "Looks like we've got a winner." Hill, still not publicly recognized as co-owner of the Derby winner, assumes that the stranger is with track security. He is not. Wooden Horse Investments, Inc., has been penetrated by a real wooden horse: an impostor who manages to get into every official winner's-circle picture. The celebration swirls toward the presentation stand, where the Governor of Kentucky is waiting. When a guard blocks his route, Billy Turner says, "Excuse me, I train this horse." The guard lets him through the ropes.

As the attention swings to the trophy presentation, John Polston leads Seattle Slew away. The groom has been fighting a winning battle to keep his emotions under control. Be cool, he has always

told himself since his early days in the streets of Baltimore. It's safer that way. No tears. But now, as he pats his Derby winner on the neck and begins to talk to him, "Hugo, you one helluva racehorse," John Polston loses the battle.

That night, while the Taylors pick up tabs for Slew Crew parties all over town, the trainer who won the 100th Derby with Cannonade lifts a glass in salute to Billy Turner. "Only one person can train a horse," says Woody Stephens at a quiet table in the Executive Inn. "Billy was his own man. He trained his own horse—and he got the roses."

But the realization still hasn't dawned on Turner, who has gone to bed early.

The next morning around 7 o'clock, while most of Louisville sleeps, Turner and Kennedy take Seattle Slew onto the track for a walk. He nips at Steamboat, a sign of exuberance, and the trainer notes that the colt is feeling fine, "as high as a Georgia pine."

Seattle Slew, the first great-grandson of Bold Ruler to win the Kentucky Derby, continued a domination of the race by that sire's descendants begun in 1970.

Six of the last eight Derbies, through 1977, have now been won by sons (one), grandsons (four) or great-grandsons (one) of the famous breeding stallion who died of cancer in 1971 at the age of seventeen. Bold Ruler, owned by the Phipps family, led the sire list (based on money earned by sons and daughters) for eight straight years, more often than any other American stallion since Lexington in the nineteenth century.

At distances of up to about a mile and an eighth, the maximum range for a majority of American stakes races, Bold Ruler's offspring were devastating. But the doubters used to say the Bold Rulers couldn't go a mile and a quarter. And until Secretariat succeeded in 1973, no son of Bold Ruler had ever won the Kentucky Derby. Bold Lad was tenth in 1965, Stupendous fourth in 1966, and Successor sixth in 1967.

Like Bold Ruler himself, who finished fourth in the 1957 Derby after Eddie Arcaro tried to rate him (i.e., restrain him) early in the race, many of his sons and daughters had a reputation for being so headstrong they could not relax unless they had the lead. But his grandsons have provided a strong vindication of Bold Ruler bloodlines at longer distances, winning four Derbies so far in this decade: Dust Commander (by Bold Commander) in 1970, Cannonade (by Bold Bidder) in 1974, Foolish Pleasure (by What a Pleasure) in 1975, and Bold Forbes (by Irish Castle) in 1976. Seattle Slew's sire, Bold Reasoning, was sired by Boldnesian, a son of Bold Ruler. Run Dusty Run, the runner-up in the 1977 Derby, also is a great-grandson of Bold Ruler, his sire being Dust Commander.

In a few hours, the whole Slew Crew will fly back to New York with the horse on a cargo plane. Clean-up crews will start clearing the Derby Day debris from infield and stands. And Smiley Adams, trainer of Run Dusty Run, will say of Seattle Slew, "He's a nice colt, but he won't win no Triple Crown."

The track is quiet now, though, almost silent. Kennedy thinks of the April day barely a year earlier, the day when Turner said, "We

The Preakness

Jean Cruguet and Slew's owners
conferring in the paddock
before the Belmont Stakes

A 28,127-TO-1 SHOT

In his race for the Triple Crown, Seattle Slew had to contend with more potential challengers than any of the nine previous winners. He was only one of 28,127 registered Thoroughbreds—a record number—foaled in North America during 1974. Of that group, 13,828 were colts and 14,299 were fillies.

Sir Barton, the 1919 winner, came from a 1916 crop of about 2000 foals, and Citation, who won the crown in 1948, was one of 5800 foaled in 1945. Secretariat, whose 1973 Triple Crown sweep was the first in twenty-five years, emerged from a 1970 class of 25,000. Man o' War, believed by many to be the greatest racehorse of all time (he won the 1920 Preakness and Belmont Stakes but was not entered in the Derby), was one of only 1680 foals born in 1917, a record low due to the First World War and a conservative attitude on the part of breeders.

Since 1953, when 9062 foals were registered with the New York-based Jockey Club, the annual number has more than tripled. The heavier demand for racehorses has resulted from an increasing reliance on pari-mutuel gambling as a source of state tax revenue, and more horses are racing today than ever before. Although most of the Thoroughbreds are still born in Kentucky, with California a very close second, every state in the country, including Alaska and Hawaii, produced at least one registered Thoroughbred in 1974, as did Puerto Rico, Cuba, Mexico, and Canada.

have to get this guy started sometime, breeze him three-eighths of a mile." And Huey had opened his mouth and taken hold of the bit and surprised them all.

Now the colt steps onto the track at the backstretch gap and stands as still as a statue, head up, gazing across the infield at the deserted grandstand. He looks and looks, as if to say, "Well, yesterday they were two daggers, now they're just two spires." Turner, on Steamboat, sees the beautiful horse he is training, and a glow comes over his face.

"Mike," he calls out to Kennedy, "do you realize what we've done? It just hit me. We won the Derby."

THE PREAKNESS

On the first Saturday of May, the theme had been red roses and "My Old Kentucky Home." On the third Saturday of May, it was black-eyed Susans and "Maryland, My Maryland." But the basic script for Act Two in racing's annual Triple Crown drama was to remain unchanged: another victory for undefeated Seattle Slew, another setback for his critics.

The skeptics had been jolted by his Derby success, but not silenced. The 102nd Preakness at Pimlico Race Course in Baltimore would be different, they insisted, because there was too much raw speed in the field for any front-runner to survive. Cormorant and J. O. Tobin, neither of whom had run in the Derby, had the kind of quickness that could draw the favorite into a suicidal early speed duel. Hadn't it happened the year before, when Bold Forbes and Honest Pleasure ran too fast too early and came up empty in the stretch?

Other doubters, among them Eddie Arcaro, continued to downgrade Slew as no more than the best of an ordinary lot of three-year-olds. But there was a slight change in Arcaro's tune. Speaking at the Alibi Breakfast, where trainers, owners, and jockeys of horses defeated in the Derby explain to the press why the outcome this time may be different, the rider of six past Preakness winners said, "We didn't see the bad start he got in the Derby, so maybe I should have called him *much* the best of an ordinary field."

Only two of the fourteen rivals Slew had beaten in Louisville, Run Dusty Run and Sir Sir, were among the eight challengers he would face in the $191,100 Preakness. Where were all the others? Answer: avoiding Seattle Slew. Lou Rondinello had decided to rest Sanhedrin for the longer Belmont Stakes. LeRoy Jolley was trying once again to restore For the Moment's confidence. And Bill O'Neill, trainer of Get the Axe, had said, "We've got to go someplace where Slew is not running."

But the fresh troops, waiting to attack like an Apache war party,

The Slew Crew
coming down
the track
on the way
to the infield
saddling enclosure
at Pimlico.

115

included two colts whose records could hardly be called ordinary. Cormorant had won seven of his nine races and J. O. Tobin, champion two-year-old of Britain the previous season, had won four out of five.

"This colt is amazing," said Johnny Adams, trainer of California-based J. O. Tobin. "He does things so easily, it's phenomenal."

Said Danny Wright, the jockey for Cormorant, "That five-furlong work in 57 3/5 my colt had at Laurel was fantastic. I couldn't believe it."

Wright injected a note of levity into the Alibi Breakfast by appearing in a pale green T-shirt with the name of his horse on the front and "Seattle Who?" on the back. When someone noted that the message couldn't upset Slew because he couldn't read, Cormorant's trainer, Jim Simpson, said, "I don't know, he's done everything else!"

But Smiley Adams, the peppery trainer of Run Dusty Run, was conceding nothing. He was still unconvinced that Slew had won the Derby "ridden out," a term meaning without need of serious urging.

"Ridden out?" Smiley had bellowed, drawing laughs from his stablehands. "He was ridden out all right—with the stick on his ass all the way from the quarter pole to the finish."

If the equine cast for the Preakness was largely different, so was the Slew Crew marquee. Jim and Sally Hill, emerging from the shadows, were now publicly much more than just the vet and the vet's wife. They were sharing equal billing with the Taylors as co-owners of Seattle Slew. Even before the Derby, Dr. Hill had begun wondering whether he should declare his association with Wooden Horse Investments, Inc. It wasn't that he particularly wanted to be in the limelight. If anything, he had always tended to shy away from reporters and the publicity they generated. But the anonymity of his role bothered him. A special twenty-six-page Derby section in a Louisville paper had mentioned him only once, as the man who had recommended the colt's purchase. A horse magazine had called him Dr. Jim Smith, and Sally had been referred to as Barbara Hill.

"Here was a horse I thought might be one of the best of all time," Hill would explain later, "and the watchdog, Lance, was getting more recognition than I was."

Three days after the Derby, he called several prominent sports columnists and notified them of the Wooden Horse setup. The New York State Racing and Wagering Board looked into the situation of his ownership of the horse but eventually decided that he must give up his veterinary practice at New York tracks as long as he held an interest in Seattle Slew and other horses racing there. Information now began coming out about the newly revealed co-owners. The public learned, for example, that Hill had worked on ranches, roped cattle, ridden in rodeos, and, since his boyhood days in Fort Myers, Florida, sailed boats. And that Sally Hill, the Alabama girl he met at Auburn University during his veterinary studies, was the daughter of an Air Force colonel and the niece of Sanders Russell, the harness driver who had won the Hambletonian with A.C.'s Viking.

Hill was still Slew's vet, though, and the immediate concern at Pimlico was the firm-packed hardness of the racing surface. To minimize any possible damage to the feet, it was decided to race the colt on Butazolidin for the first time in his career. Although this anti-inflammatory analgesic, which some horsemen call a "super aspirin," is prohibited from use in racing in some states, it is allowed in Maryland. However, a trainer must stipulate two days before the race, when entries close, whether a horse will be running with or without bute.

The day before entries closed, the Slew Crew was jarred by the news that Susan Small had been badly injured at a Pennsylvania farm where she had been breaking yearlings and young two-year-olds for them. A horse had flipped over and struck her with its head while falling, crushing her ribs and part of one lung. Susan's father, Burley Cocks, was the trainer for whom Billy Turner had once ridden steeplechasers, and the young woman was a close friend of the Hills. (She would be hospitalized, under intensive care, for a month.)

"This kind of puts the horse race into perspective," said Hill. "You realize how unimportant it is compared to Susan's life."

Turner had tried to keep Seattle Slew relaxed between the Derby and the Preakness. To take the youthful exuberance out of him, the trainer worked his colt seven furlongs in 1:22 4/5 at Belmont Park the Sunday before the race. Slew had his final blowout, three furlongs at Pimlico, the day before the Preakness.

"I can do anything I want," said Jean Cruguet, without sounding

117

like a braggart. "I can go to the lead or take him back. Every time this horse runs, you have new customers, which is okay with me."

The largest crowd in the history of Pimlico, 77,346, jammed the old track on Preakness Day. Attendance surpassed the previous record of 75,216, set at the 100th Preakness, and was well above the turnout of 61,657 that saw Secretariat win the 1973 Preakness en route to his Triple Crown sweep. Until Secretariat, Pimlico had never had a crowd as large as 50,000. As usual, the color motif was yellow and black, from the clothes worn by Susan Rosenberg, Miss Preakness, to the blanket of flowers draped around the winner. All the black-eyed Susans, of course, were make-believe. Since the state flower doesn't bloom in Maryland until July, a Baltimore florist takes thousands of yellow daisies and dyes the centers black with shoe polish. Appropriately, the traditional Preakness colors were the same as Seattle Slew's.

If the infield crowd was a little more sober than the one at the Derby, and a little more knowledgeable about horses, the carnival atmosphere was the same. In addition to marching bands, the day-long musical program offered a choice of rock (Appaloosa, Blue Meanies, Total Reaction), country-bluegrass, and Dixieland. Through the day, horseplayers debated the Preakness issue. Would Cormorant, on the rail in the No. 1 post, exploit the track "bias" that in recent weeks had favored horses who could take the lead along the inside? Would Seattle Slew, from the No. 8 post, have trouble getting to the front? Would he wash out in the paddock again? Come out of the gate sideways? Ruin himself in a speed duel with Cormorant or J. O. Tobin? Then the bettors gave their answer. They made Slew an odds-on favorite at 2 to 5.

The fans turned out to be accurate prophets. Slew was calm in the outdoor paddock area, alert in the gate, and completely dominant once the race began. As expected, he and Cormorant hooked up immediately in a speed duel that carried them far ahead of the others. But it was clear early on which jockey had the most horse under him. Wright had to urge Cormorant for speed to take the lead along the inside in the first quarter while Slew, under a tight hold by Cruguet, moved up easily to join the front-runner. Racing together, they accounted for some of the fastest fractions in Preakness history: a quarter in 22 3/5, a half in 45 3/5, six furlongs in 1:09 4/5. Then Cruguet clucked to the favorite, and

By the upper stretch, Slew had the Preakness well under control.

Seattle Slew zoomed away from Cormorant halfway through the final bend. His time for the mile was 1:34 4/5, the fastest ever run by any horse in the Preakness. And he kept going, coming home without pressure a length and a half ahead of Iron Constitution as Run Dusty Run finished third, Cormorant fourth, and J. O. Tobin fifth. His time of 1:54 2/5 for the mile and three-sixteenths, identical to Secretariat's, was the second-fastest in the 102 years of the race.

One of Cormorant's staunchest backers, William C. Phillips of the *Daily Racing Form*, was quick to salute the winner. "It would be difficult now," he wrote, "for anybody to damn Seattle Slew with the faint praise that he is the best of an ordinary lot. It would be even more difficult finding anybody to believe it."

The column ran under a headline that read "Nothing Left to Knock." But the knockers were still at work, insisting now that the mile and a half of the Belmont Stakes would surely wreck Seattle Slew's hopes for a Triple Crown. As Arcaro had argued, "To be considered great, a horse has to be able to win at a mile and a half." Could Slew go that far? The answer would come in three weeks.

119

VICTORY AT BELMONT

Billy Turner had been trying for months not to think about it. At Christmas, he hadn't even thumbed through the pages of an illustrated book on the Triple Crown given to him by a friend. He knew the honor roll as well as he knew his own name: Sir Barton, Gallant Fox, Omaha, War Admiral, Whirlaway, Count Fleet, Assault, Citation, Secretariat. But Turner didn't want to think about the Triple Crown, because he knew the colt he was training had a solid chance to win it.

Now the young trainer had to think about it. If Seattle Slew could go a mile and a half, if he could win the 109th Belmont Stakes, the impossible dream would come true. Thoroughbred racing's first undefeated Triple Crown champion. It was all within reach now, the brass ring on the world's biggest merry-go-round. For a long time, Turner had been convinced that the dark brown colt he still called Huey was the fastest horse in America. And all along, the question in the back of his mind had been: How do you get the fastest horse in America to go a mile and a half?

"Stretch this colt out that far," he had told himself, "and he'll be one of the greatest horses in history. If you can make that speed last a mile and a half, it's unbeatable."

The strategy for the Belmont was clear: relaxation. Too many good horses had come apart like a ball of yarn by going too fast too early in the so-called "test of the champion." Get Huey to relax, to wait until Cruguet asked him for speed, and he could run all day. A training routine of long, leisurely galloping was begun. The slow gallops, some of them as much as three or four miles in length, would dull the colt's speed and build his endurance, like the long roadwork a fighter does before a big bout. They would also help him recover from the jarring he had taken in the Preakness on Pimlico's hard racing surface. He had come out of that race muscle-sore for the first time in his career.

By now, Turner was beginning to feel the loneliness of the long-distance runner. A Triple Crown campaign, he knew, was the

Mickey, Mike, and Karen clocking Slew's workout at Belmont a few days before the race.
Right:
Heading out
in the fog for
a workout at Belmont
on June 2.

121

Donald Carroll
holding Slew
for his bath
after the workout.

hardest assignment in racing: three tough races against the best opposition at different distances on different surfaces during the short span of five weeks. The trick, of course, was to keep a horse at his peak for all three. Of the eight horses in the last nineteen years who had gone into the Belmont with a chance to sweep the series, only Secretariat had made it.

As the days slipped past and Seattle Slew became more and more relaxed, the pressure increased for the people around him. They were all in it together, the Taylors and Hills and their troops, all exposed to the glare of publicity that had turned the colt's residence into the most-photographed barn in America.

"This is Barn 54, Belmont Park, home of Seattle Slew," television commentators would say theatrically after waving their camera crews into position inside a split-rail fence covered by rambler roses. Beds of purple petunias and yellow marigolds alongside the dark green barn gave the area a tranquil appearance. But the pressure was there, constantly.

Nine days before the race, Seattle Slew worked a mile in the early-morning fog. Turner, riding Steamboat, dropped Slew and Jean Cruguet off at the mile pole, then rushed back toward the finish line in the opposite direction as fast as the broad-beamed stable pony could gallop. They made it just in time to catch sight of the colt as he emerged from the fog around the eighth pole, going strongly and easily. Back at the barn, when somebody from the press complained about vital workout information being obscured, the trainer showed that he still hadn't lost his sense of humor. "We do a lot of things on the racetrack in the fog, you know," he noted, reflecting racing's traditional intrigue. "I caught him in 1:38 and two-fifths." Then he rapped his knuckles against the side of the barn and said, "Knock on wood, the horse is doing fine. No problems."

John Polston, sponging Seattle Slew with soapy water from a plastic bucket, laughed when Turner fished a roll of mints from his pocket and asked, "Anyone want a Rolaid?" The groom rinsed the colt off, put a cooler on him, and prepared to turn him over to Donald Carroll to be walked. Just before he did, Polston stepped back like a proud father and gave Slew a gentle slap on the rump.

Later, taking a break in the track cafeteria, Polston smiled to himself when a loud-mouthed exercise rider at the next table bellowed, "I still think he's a paper tiger. He hasn't run against real class yet." A sign on the wall advised the clientele: "Eat Your Betting Money, But Never Bet Your Eating Money." It was strange, Polston thought, how one really good horse could change your gambling habits. One time a long way back, he had put $400 to win on an old horse he was rubbing that had bad ankles and a lot of courage. It was the only time in his life he had ever bet more than $100 at a racetrack. He remembered standing at the rail at Belmont and feeling his legs almost cave in under him when Arabian Spy came home in front at odds of nearly 10 to 1. But this was different, for himself and Carroll and Mike Kennedy and all the others. You could go a lifetime without getting a horse half as good as Seattle Slew. This pony had come along and taken them all to the top.

A week before the Belmont, John Esposito used a paint brush to let the world know where he stood. He painted the white picket fence outside Esposito's Tavern in alternate slats of black and yellow. Seattle Slew's colors. After all, Billy Turner had started coming to Espo's as an eighteen-year-old steeplechase jockey.

"I've been with this horse all the way," the bartender explained when some of his customers wondered if he shouldn't have waited

until after the race. "He'll leave 'em like a freight train leaving hobos."

This wasn't just any horse, Esposito knew. This was the dark brown colt Turner had told him about the previous summer when he said he had a steamroller ready to cut loose that would make them all take notice. "It's Huey," he remembered the trainer saying. "You'll get this real name when he runs." If Esposito had no doubts, neither did the Squirrel. After the Derby, the former exercise rider made a bet with Turner involving the trainer's "lucky" tweed hunt-meet cap. If Slew won the Triple Crown, the Squirrel would get the cap. If the colt failed, the Squirrel would "walk hots" for Turner—lead horses around the barn to cool them out—every Sunday for five months.

For Paula Turner, the Triple Crown countdown had already produced a bonus. She had finally met Walter Farley, author of the *Black Stallion* books, the man who wrote the dreams she had lived in for as long as she could remember. She had meant to ask Farley how the boy in his story had got the New York Racing Association to let his horse run without papers, but it didn't matter now.

On the Tuesday before the Belmont, Seattle Slew was given his last serious workout: six furlongs in 1:11 3/5, with Cruguet up. The only remaining tuneup, a three-furlong blowout, would take place the day before the race with Kennedy in the saddle.

While Slew prospered, Lou Rondinello paced the shed row of his Darby Dan barn like a Captain Ahab pursuing an equine Moby Dick. "Maybe we'll make it this time," the trainer of Sanhedrin said as he discussed strategy. "If that other horse puts in a real fast mile, it's not going to take a hell of a run to get past him. Nobody knows for sure which horses can go a mile and a half."

But Cruguet wasn't worried about Sanhedrin. He called the stretch-runner a "Johnny-come-lately," and he showed little fear of the others, either. Smiley Adams, offering no excuses for the Derby and Preakness, had Run Dusty Run back for another try. And Iron Constitution and Sir Sir would be in the field, too. But the rest of the cast was new.

One of the newcomers, Spirit Level, was owned by Mrs. Penny Ringquist, who as Mrs. Penny Tweedy had directed Secretariat to his Triple Crown sweep for Meadow Stable.

"Winning is always wonderful," Mrs. Ringquist said at the press breakfast after entries were taken, "whether your horse is ex-

pected to win or whether the victory sneaks up on you. We're hoping, like everybody else."

Said Cruguet, privately, "The first one gonna try to catch me gonna die."

"I don't think there are any heroes left, are there?" ventured John Russell, trainer for the Phipps family. "I think they'll ignore Slew and go for second place."

In a sense, Seattle Slew would be running as much against the legend of Secretariat as against real opponents. But several days of heavy rain had left the track muddy, and there was no chance the colt could come close to the record time of 2 minutes 24 seconds set by Secretariat on a lightning-fast surface that had produced a flock of records in the weeks leading up to the 1973 Belmont. Secretariat had won by a dazzling thirty-one lengths, but as Cruguet pointed out, "If a jockey in Europe wins by more than three or four lengths, he's considered a bad rider. You have to think of the handicap races, where lengths mean extra pounds."

Once again, as it had at the Derby and Preakness, the box-office appeal of Seattle Slew did wonders for the gate. Despite the impact of two hundred off-track-betting shops in the New York City area, 71,026 people turned out at the track under clearing skies on June 11 for the $181,800 Belmont. It was the second-largest crowd in Belmont Park's venerable history, exceeded only by the 82,694 who saw Canonero II's unsuccessful Triple Crown bid in 1971 before OTB began eroding attendance.

Cruguet's confidence was evident from the moment he arrived at the track with his wife and daughter at 11 a.m. Denise and nine-year-old Leslie each wore a white carnation, the flower used in the traditional blanket that goes to the winner of the Belmont. Cruguet carried Seattle Slew's black and yellow racing silks, fresh from the dry cleaner's, in a cellophane wrapping on a coat hanger. John Gorham, the man known as Carwash, waved to him and moved toward the car with a bucket of soapy detergent. In the jockey room, a newspaper headline taped to a shelf above Cruguet's bench reflected the Frenchman's new status. It read "Jean Cruguet Is a Somebody."

Spectators in shoulder-to-shoulder rows thirty deep jammed the terraces overlooking the paddock to catch a glimpse of him. Near the railing, a group of teen-age girls displayed a homemade poster: "We Believe Seattle Slew Can Do!" Others wore T-shirts inscribed with the horse's name. But their hero would be late, so late that post time for the nationally televised race would have to be delayed five minutes. Cars parked illegally in the stable area had blocked his usual route to the track, and a detour had to be taken. In addition, Billy Turner had gotten Slew so relaxed that he stopped at every crossing in the paths. Finally he arrived, eyes flashing, his dark mahogany coat gleaming in the sunlight. Nine months earlier he had come into this same paddock as a first-time starter with a noncommittal *Daily Racing Form* comment of "Begins Career Today." Now he was the star of the show, and the final act of the drama was about to be played out.

From the call of "Put your riders up," the impossible dream moved in what seemed like slow motion toward its conclusion: black and yellow silks, the same colors carried by Man o' War, moving out of the paddock past the ancient white pine, its branches held together by wire supports, a tree that had seen

every Triple Crown winner begin the final walk to the post; past the bronze of Secretariat; onto the track while the band played "Sidewalks of New York"; up to the starting gate; and then into an immediate lead when the doors of the stalls banged open.

Jean Cruguet knew it was going to be easy before they had gone half a mile. Slew was practically walking, relaxing perfectly, yet he continued to lead. Billy Turner, too, knew the battle was over as soon as he saw the slow early fractions on the tote-board teletimer: a quarter in 24 3/5, a half in 48 2/5, six furlongs in 1:14. That was about as slow as his colt could be conned into running, slower than he would normally run in a morning workout. And still, the riders of the other horses had not dared to attack. Turner had gone to a bar on the ground level of the grandstand a few minutes before the start and ordered a double vodka tonic.

"Get in line, buddy," the bartender had told him.

"Hey," Mike Kennedy had protested, "he trains Seattle Slew. Give him a drink."

When he saw the six-furlong time, Turner said to no one in particular, "Let him run, Jean." As expected, Sanhedrin made a big late challenge, perfectly timed by Jorge Velasquez, which brought him up alongside the leader just before they reached the quarter pole near the top of the stretch. But Cruguet just chirped to Seattle Slew, and it was over. He was four lengths in front as they straightened away into the stretch. The brass ring was waiting. With a sixteenth of a mile to go, Chester Taylor turned to his son and said, "Oh my gosh, Mick, I better get back to the barn. I just remembered, I left Lance in Slew's stall."

But there was one final flourish to come, an unforgettable Gallic touch by Cruguet that would give some of Slew's backers a scare but turn the moment into pure magic for most of them. Twenty yards from the finish, with his horse in full stride, Cruguet stood up in the stirrups, raised his right arm over his head, and jubilantly waved his whip to the crowd in a victory salute. It was a wild thing to do, impulsive and reckless—and magnificent. Nobody else had ever done it, but no other Triple Crown winner had ever crossed the line undefeated.

"Thank you, Jean," Paula Turner would say to the jockey later. "That's when I realized what Huey had done, and what made it so different."

"If Slew can carry him, I can, too!"

Billy Turner broke a precedent for his Triple Crown champion and came into the winner's circle at Belmont.

EPILOGUE

A rooster saluted the new day. Seattle Slew was already wide awake, finishing breakfast in his stall at Barn 54. While his people were celebrating, racing's first undefeated Triple Crown winner had slept like a baby.

But now the rhythm of the backstretch was beginning to resume. Stablehands rubbed the sleep from their eyes. Even on Sunday, there were horses to be cared for, dreams to be dreamed. As Billy Turner put it the morning after the Belmont, "The game goes on." On the breeding farms, yearlings were filling out and new foals were tagging along beside their mothers. And in the stable area at Belmont Park, crash-helmeted exercise riders were steering horses along sandy paths toward the track. At Barn 54, though, the pressure was off. Seattle Slew would do nothing more today than walk, graze, and pose for pictures. When his trainer showed up, a little later than usual, it was obvious the troops had returned to their old mood of cheerful irreverence.

"You're fired, Turner," Sam said, shaking her head. "Didn't I warn you about getting to work on time?"

Other members of the Slew Crew arrived later, among them the outfit's newest and youngest stablehands: four-year-old Jamie Hill and his nine-year-old sister, Brandon, the children of Jim and Sally Hill. There was talk about Seattle Slew's getting a long vacation, talk about running him as a four-year-old if he stayed sound. Even Steamboat, the brown and white stable pony, seemed more relaxed as he slouched against the side of the barn and quietly moved his head up and down in an effort to loosen the snaps on the tether that held him.

Billy Turner fished a crumpled letter out of his pocket and, laughing, handed it to Mike Kennedy. "Dear Turner," it began, "you punk! How dare you say the track was fast for Secretariat's Belmont? No, my punk friend, the track wasn't fast. Secretariat was fast. If your horse had to face Secretariat, Damascus,

Buckpasser, Kelso, or Dr. Fager, he'd be slaughtered. I demand an apology!"

"How do you answer something like that?" asked Turner.

"You don't," Kennedy said. "We know what Huey can do, but he's never going to race those others. And what difference does it make, anyway? They're all great horses."

It was unreal, Turner thought. Here was a colt who had never lost, a colt who had won the Triple Crown and laughed all the way back to the barn. Why should a horse like that need an apology? Secretariat was great, sure, but he lost three times before his Triple Crown and two times afterward. Was the breeding industry afraid that Slew could be an economic threat to Secretariat, whose stud fee was $100,000 and whose yearlings were averaging $300,000 at auction?

At least one of the critics, Eddie Arcaro, was taking a far more charitable view. He had watched the Belmont on television from his home in Miami, and the wire services reported his reaction: "I don't think you earn the honor of being called 'great' just by having people say you're great, but this horse has all the qualities of greatness. He has to do more, though."

A few of the diehards were still arguing that Seattle Slew had run against "very mediocre" opposition. But some of the most respected trainers in the business, men like Woody Stephens and Allen Jerkens, were calling the colt great. And a look at the past performances of the "mediocre" rivals Slew had faced gave little support to the critics. Four of his top opponents—Run Dusty Run, Cormorant, J. O. Tobin, and For the Moment—had finished first or second in thirty-seven of their forty-one races before they ran in the Derby, Preakness, or Belmont.

"An extraordinary horse," said Pat Lynch, a New York Racing Association executive who has seen a lot of good ones. "His controlled power is the thing that impresses me. He'll give you two or three separate responses during a race. Most horses have only one."

Beyond the immediate gold and glory of the hour, of course, the unblemished Triple Crown sweep had long-range implications of major importance. The $717,720 earned by the former $17,500 yearling in his nine-race march to fame was minor compared to Seattle Slew's value as a breeding stallion. His young owners would be weighing syndication offers of as much as twelve million dollars. They, too, like Billy Turner, would be getting increasing amounts of mail. And so would John Esposito. A few days later, the bartender would show customers a wire-service dispatch a friend in Saratoga had mailed him.

"It was 12:30 a.m. Sunday," the story began, "when the Taylors left Esposito's, an ordinary tavern across the street from the backstretch in Belmont Park. It was hardly the place you'd expect to see the owners of a horse who several hours earlier made racing history."

Esposito was indignant. "What do they mean by 'ordinary' tavern? This place has never been ordinary. We've had millionaries coming in here for years."

Of all the mail, though, the heaviest volume was addressed to "Seattle Slew, Belmont Park, New York." Huey, the ugly-duckling colt who had grown into a swan, was averaging fifty fan letters a day. One admirer, a young girl from South Carolina, sent a signed blank check. An accompanying note, with the word "pictures" scrawled across it, explained that her bank account contained $12.80.

Now, on the day after he won the Triple Crown, Slew was taking it easy. But he could see other horses moving along the paths toward the track. One of them, an unraced two-year-old, tugged at the bit as he marched forward on springy legs. He was a big, awkward-looking colt. But he had a proud eye, and his ears were up, listening to the sound of hoofbeats on the training track.

"Easy, daddy," his exercise rider crooned to him. "You gonna get your chance."

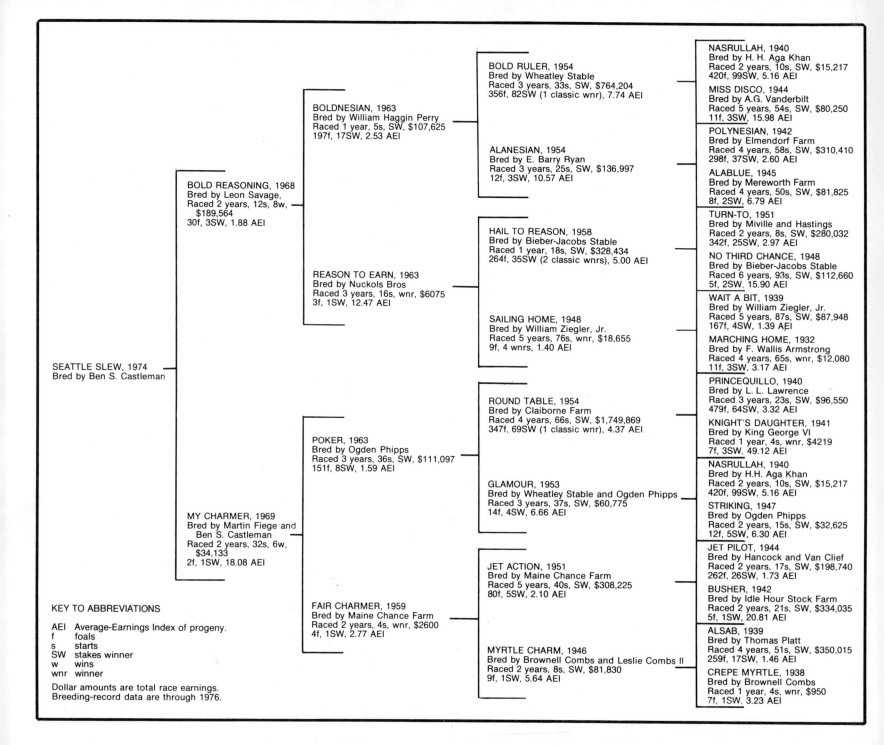

SEATTLE SLEW, 1974
Bred by Ben S. Castleman

BOLD REASONING, 1968
Bred by Leon Savage,
Raced 2 years, 12s, 8w,
$189,564
30f, 3SW, 1.88 AEI

BOLDNESIAN, 1963
Bred by William Haggin Perry
Raced 1 year, 5s, SW, $107,625
197f, 17SW, 2.53 AEI

BOLD RULER, 1954
Bred by Wheatley Stable
Raced 3 years, 33s, SW, $764,204
356f, 82SW (1 classic wnr), 7.74 AEI

NASRULLAH, 1940
Bred by H. H. Aga Khan
Raced 2 years, 10s, SW, $15,217
420f, 99SW, 5.16 AEI

MISS DISCO, 1944
Bred by A.G. Vanderbilt
Raced 5 years, 54s, SW, $80,250
11f, 3SW, 15.98 AEI

ALANESIAN, 1954
Bred by E. Barry Ryan
Raced 3 years, 25s, SW, $136,997
12f, 3SW, 10.57 AEI

POLYNESIAN, 1942
Bred by Elmendorf Farm
Raced 4 years, 58s, SW, $310,410
298f, 37SW, 2.60 AEI

ALABLUE, 1945
Bred by Mereworth Farm
Raced 4 years, 50s, SW, $81,825
8f, 2SW, 6.79 AEI

REASON TO EARN, 1963
Bred by Nuckols Bros
Raced 3 years, 16s, wnr, $6075
3f, 1SW, 12.47 AEI

HAIL TO REASON, 1958
Bred by Bieber-Jacobs Stable
Raced 1 year, 18s, SW, $328,434
264f, 35SW (2 classic wnrs), 5.00 AEI

TURN-TO, 1951
Bred by Miville and Hastings
Raced 2 years, 8s, SW, $280,032
342f, 25SW, 2.97 AEI

NO THIRD CHANCE, 1948
Bred by Bieber-Jacobs Stable
Raced 6 years, 93s, SW, $112,660
5f, 2SW, 15.90 AEI

SAILING HOME, 1948
Bred by William Ziegler, Jr.
Raced 5 years, 76s, wnr, $18,655
9f, 4 wnrs, 1.40 AEI

WAIT A BIT, 1939
Bred by William Ziegler, Jr.
Raced 5 years, 87s, SW, $87,948
167f, 4SW, 1.39 AEI

MARCHING HOME, 1932
Bred by F. Wallis Armstrong
Raced 4 years, 65s, wnr, $12,080
11f, 3SW, 3.17 AEI

MY CHARMER, 1969
Bred by Martin Fiege and
Ben S. Castleman
Raced 2 years, 32s, 6w,
$34,133
2f, 1SW, 18.08 AEI

POKER, 1963
Bred by Ogden Phipps
Raced 3 years, 36s, SW, $111,097
151f, 8SW, 1.59 AEI

ROUND TABLE, 1954
Bred by Claiborne Farm
Raced 4 years, 66s, SW, $1,749,869
347f, 69SW (1 classic wnr), 4.37 AEI

PRINCEQUILLO, 1940
Bred by L. L. Lawrence
Raced 3 years, 23s, SW, $96,550
479f, 64SW, 3.32 AEI

KNIGHT'S DAUGHTER, 1941
Bred by King George VI
Raced 1 year, 4s, wnr, $4219
7f, 3SW, 49.12 AEI

GLAMOUR, 1953
Bred by Wheatley Stable and Ogden Phipps
Raced 3 years, 37s, SW, $60,775
14f, 4SW, 6.66 AEI

NASRULLAH, 1940
Bred by H.H. Aga Khan
Raced 2 years, 10s, SW, $15,217
420f, 99SW, 5.16 AEI

STRIKING, 1947
Bred by Ogden Phipps
Raced 2 years, 15s, SW, $32,625
12f, 5SW, 6.30 AEI

FAIR CHARMER, 1959
Bred by Maine Chance Farm
Raced 2 years, 4s, wnr, $2600
4f, 1SW, 2.77 AEI

JET ACTION, 1951
Bred by Maine Chance Farm
Raced 5 years, 40s, SW, $308,225
80f, 5SW, 2.10 AEI

JET PILOT, 1944
Bred by Hancock and Van Clief
Raced 2 years, 17s, SW, $198,740
262f, 26SW, 1.73 AEI

BUSHER, 1942
Bred by Idle Hour Stock Farm
Raced 2 years, 21s, SW, $334,035
5f, 1SW, 20.81 AEI

MYRTLE CHARM, 1946
Bred by Brownell Combs and Leslie Combs II
Raced 2 years, 8s, SW, $81,830
9f, 1SW, 5.64 AEI

ALSAB, 1939
Bred by Thomas Platt
Raced 4 years, 51s, SW, $350,015
259f, 17SW, 1.46 AEI

CREPE MYRTLE, 1938
Bred by Brownell Combs
Raced 1 year, 4s, wnr, $950
7f, 1SW, 3.23 AEI

KEY TO ABBREVIATIONS

AEI   Average-Earnings Index of progeny.
f   foals
s   starts
SW   stakes winner
w   wins
wnr   winner

Dollar amounts are total race earnings.
Breeding-record data are through 1976.